D0759523

POGROM

POGROM

A Novel of Armenian History

Aleksandr Shaginyan

Translated by David Floyd

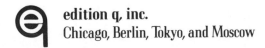
edition q, inc.
Chicago, Berlin, Tokyo, and Moscow

© 1994 by edition q, inc.

Library of Congress Cataloging-In-Publication Data:

Shaginyan, Aleksandr.
    Pogrom : a novel of Armenian history / Aleksandr Shaginyan ;
translated by David Floyd.
        p.   cm.
    ISBN 1-883695-00-7
    1. Sumgait (Azerbaijan)—History—Fiction.   2. Massacres—
Azerbaijan—Sumgait—Fiction.   I. Title.
PG3487.A513P64   1994
891.73'44—dc20   93-43509
                                                                CIP

All rights reserved. This book or any part thereof may not be reproduced, stored
in a retrieval system, or transmitted in any form or by any means, electronic,
mechanical, photocopying, recording, or otherwise, without prior written
permission of the publisher.

Manufactured in the United States of America

In memory of my dear Anaid, Bella, and Vartan

CONTENTS

EDITOR'S NOTE

L et it not be misunderstood: This book does not claim to be a balanced, neutral report on the massacre in Sumgait. To the contrary, it is a subjective and biased account of events. It is the cry of a soul in torment, the attempt by one writer to ease the pain and anger over crimes committed against his fellow countrymen. Author Aleksandr Shaginyan has written this book not out of coolly detached reason, but out of a heartrending passion for his subject. The Armenians have too often been the victims of brutal repression and extermination while the rest of the world has averted its eyes and gone on with its power politics as usual.

The murder of the people of Sumgait in 1988 is a historical fact, even if there were no televised images to create international concern, no CNN cameras to capture events as they happened. The reason these people died is equally well known: They were Armenians. The identity of their murderers is known, too: Azerbaijanis. Because they are unable to find a humane solution to the problem of dividing up a small piece of our great earth—the region of Nagorno-Karabakh—and live together in peace, they instead kill each other off. It is a solution based not on tolerance and understanding but on intolerance and hate.

Perhaps an Azerbaijani could write a similar book, with the roles of perpetrator and victim reversed. The madness of what we refer to as "ethnic cleansing" is not something that has befallen only one nation, one tribe, one race—a fact that does not diminish the crime.

Confronted with the shocking and horrible images and reports coming out of Serbia, Bosnia, Herzegovina, Croatia, Somalia, Georgia, Kurdistan, Gaza, Lebanon, Haiti—and Armenia and Azerbaijan—politicians and citizens of all countries not directly involved in the conflict are asking themselves: Which is the right side, and which the wrong? With whom should we sympathize? Whom should we support? The discussions and debates, the cease-fire negotiations, and general assemblies are dominated by political, religious, racial, territorial, and historical arguments, arguments that have gained nothing from having been used for centuries now.

Like Franz Werfel before him, Aleksandr Shaginyan illustrates, with his fictive account of another brutal chapter of Armenian history, the reality of the suffering and the cruelty of the individual tragedy behind the cynical maneuvering of the political parties, the daily newspaper and television reports of "disturbances" or "continued outbreaks of fighting" in this or that part of the world. And in doing so, he answers in his own way the many questions concerning justice and injustice. Whoever kills another, regardless in the name of which god, which regime, which race, or which party, commits a crime against humanity.

—HENNO LOHMEYER

ONE

They burst into a ward in the maternity home, stabbed two women in their beds and raped a woman doctor they took to be Armenian.

One of the women was so terrified that she went into labor. The pain made her cry out and draw up her knees. Her blanket slid off the bed, and revealed the head of a child emerging from her body.

"Just look at that now!" exclaimed Maksud, leader of the gang. "Another damned Armenian creeping into the world!"

His friends grinned.

"Let's help it on its way," he said. He put his hairy hands between the woman's legs and pulled the child out by its head.

The woman let out a scream.

"She's not Armenian," said the doctor, lying on the floor, her skirt in tatters, with a groan. "She's an Ossetian."

One of the gang, known as Khobot, prodded her with a pointed stick and said reproachfully, "Why do you have to tell lies?"

Maksud held the whimpering infant up, cut the cord with one stroke of his knife, showed the child to its screaming mother and then hurled it out the window. The noise of breaking glass filled the room.

"No woman can have given birth to a monster like you," muttered an Azerbaijani woman in a bed further down the ward.

"The child's gone for a little walk," Maksud laughed, revealing a row of beautiful teeth below the thin line of his moustache.

All this took place in the town of Sumgait, in the Soviet Socialist Republic of Azerbaijan, in this century—on the twenty-seventh day of February, 1988.

One morning, just a month earlier, through the mist of a hard January frost, a plane on the regular service from Baku, the capitol of Azerbaijan, landed in Moscow's Domodedovo airport.

Following the blinking light of the airport guide-car, the plane taxied to its resting place, close to the glass-fronted airport building. As the steps were brought into position, a black Volga with a roof antenna pulled up alongside them. A man in an expensive gray overcoat and a matching gray Persian lamb hat broke away from the crowd of passengers. With a quick glance at the car's registration number, he opened the car door and said something to the driver, who nodded in agreement. The man from Baku sat in the back seat, and the car drove out of the airport through a special exit and onto the highway. The thick-necked driver accelerated sharply and headed the Volga towards Moscow.

He soon turned off the orbital road to join the Minsk highway and, ignoring all the rules of the road, headed for the Triumphal arch. The high-rise buildings on Kalinin Avenue came into sight, then the Riding School. Finally, leaving behind Dzerzhinsky Square (the man from Baku shuddered slightly at the sight of its main building, KGB headquarters), the car came to a halt at the last entrance to the somber edifice on the Old Square that housed the Central Committee of the Communist Party of the Soviet Union.

"Just a moment," said the driver, without looking back. He ran across to the entrance gate, next to which stood a guard in a fur-lined uniform coat, with the blue trimmings of the KGB and a gun holster hanging from his belt. With a friendly nod to the guard, the driver disappeared into the entrance.

The man from Baku felt rather awkward. He withdrew even deeper into the back seat, so people leaving the building would not see his face.

It was no more than a minute before the driver shot out of the entrance again. "All in order," he said as he opened the car door, and it was only then that the man from Baku noticed what penetrating eyes he had.

The driver put the Volga into reverse, spun it around on the spot, and with a screech of tires raced off back the way they had come—past the Lyubyanka again, down towards the Riding School and on along Kutuzov avenue. At the Minsk department store, where there was a line nearly a half-mile long for something in short supply, the driver turned onto the Rublyov highway. It was only then that the man from Baku realized that he was being taken out of town, to the pleasant outskirts of Moscow, where most of the country houses belonging to top Party and government officials were found.

After covering another six miles, the Volga turned off on an asphalt side road, closed to the public, and drove first through an attractive beech wood, then through a dense fir plantation, stopping at a set of high, firmly closed gates. A security man in civilian clothes appeared immediately. He looked into the car, cast his eyes over the man from Baku and gave a sign. The green gates rolled aside and a two-story house, also painted green and with a glassed-in veranda, came into view.

The man whom the Baku visitor had come to think of as Big Man No. 2 turned out to be short in stature, with hanging cheeks and close-cut graying hair. In real life he bore little resemblance to the many portraits of him that appeared in the press.

Big Man No. 2 met the man from Baku in the doorway of a spacious study with a massive desk and with bookshelves lining the walls. The guest had time to take in the fact that the books were all enormous collections of Lenin's works and other Communist classics, bound in luxurious leather.

"So here I am," said the man from Baku, a servile expression on his face. "On your instructions."

Big Man No. 2 cast his eyes around his study in a meaningful way. His guest nodded in understanding. "Unfortunately I cannot be as hospitable a host here as you are down there." With a vague gesture the Big Man gave his guest to understand that he did not wish to say aloud the place where his guest had come from. "I have only an hour to spare—then I have to be at a meeting of the Politburo." He took the man from Baku by the arm and led him into the garden, and did not say another word until they were outside the house.

However, his precautions were quite ineffective. Two hundred yards away, on the other side of the garden fence, an observer perched in the fork of a tall tree had already picked them up on his omnidirectional microphones.

"Can you guess why you've been summoned to Moscow?" the Big Man asked at last.

"I'm all ears," said the guest, keeping a respectful half-step behind his host.

"First of all, I will bring you up to date briefly on the country's situation as it is today." The Big Man joined his hands behind his back and walked slowly down the path, which had been cleared of snow. "It is, as you know, very complicated. One might even say revolting. I am going to be extremely frank with you."

The listener in the tree pricked up his ears and adjusted his headphones so as not to miss a single word that was said.

"With his liberal tricks, the present General Secretary is hacking at the very roots of the Soviet system. He's overdone it. Today even many of the KGB are beginning to understand this, although it was they who produced him and it was with their help that he advanced so quickly to occupy the key position in the country. They saw that Brezhnev couldn't last long, that the stupid Chernenko would soon be carried off in a box, and that Andropov himself was mortally sick . . . "

They turned off onto a side path, winding between the snow drifts. They were surrounded by fir trees, the branches piled high with snow that had frozen in the cold air.

"Our great and powerful country, the first country in the world in which socialism has triumphed, is falling to pieces like an old rug. The Tatars are starting to grumble, the Armenians are beginning to shout about their Nagorno-Karabakh, but most important is the unrest in the Baltic republics, because they have a frontier directly with the West, to which they are obviously drawn. Incidentally, our own fellow, you know, he also is out to impress the wonderful West with his tricks." The Big Man gave a wry grin. "You see how he's trying to ingratiate himself with world public opinion—he'd like to win a Nobel Prize."

The sound of snow being crunched beneath their feet caused the listener to adjust the background noise.

"The Politburo is literally snowed under with letters from anxious Party members and non-Party patriots. They are alarmed by this irresponsible policy. And it's as if this fellow and the people around him had been let off the chain!" Big Man No. 2 struck the palm of his hand violently with his fist. "We've had enough. The country needs firm rule. Without any Stalinist excesses, of course. But with strong leaders in charge of the Party."

"You are our only hope," said the man from Baku in a flattering tone.

The Big Man frowned. "There's no need for that. I don't like it."

"I'm sorry."

"But for there to be a possible change of leadership the country needs a jolly good shake-up"—the host now switched to the question which had in fact brought the man from Baku on the long journey to Moscow. "The people have got to get a glimpse of the abyss into which an irresponsible policy can lead the country. The bitter conflict between the Armenians and your compatriots over Nagorno-Karabakh will demonstrate just how deep that abyss is. Especially since Azerbaijan's demands on Nagorno-Karabakh are just."

"Throughout history it always belonged to us," the man from Baku interjected.

"I don't know what history says," the Big Man muttered in a tone of annoyance, "but that's what I think. Where would we be if everyone who felt like it was to change frontiers fixed by law?"

"Yes," said the man from Baku indignantly.

"Soon the republic of Tadjikistan would be demanding to be joined with the state of Texas!"

"You're right!" the man from Baku exclaimed with some heat. "It just takes someone to set an example and goodness only knows where we would end up!"

"I'm glad you have grasped the essence of the matter right away," commented the Big Man approvingly.

The man from Baku glowed with pleasure. His whole future career in the Party depended on his host's disposition towards him. If the Big Man eventually were to achieve the key position in the Politburo, he would, of course, not forget the loyalty and services of those who helped get him there.

"If only everybody was as quick to understand," the Big Man said with bitterness in his voice and then, wrapping his fur coat tightly around him, turned back towards the house.

In hopes of improving the quality of his recording, the listener moved on to another branch, and carelessly knocked a whole load of snow off the tree. The falling snow attracted attention. A man looked out of a window high in the attic of the house and immediately drew back.

On the front steps, Big Man No. 2 offered his hand and said gravely: "A great deal hangs on your taking decisive action. Not just the question of whether Nagorno-Karabakh belongs to Azerbaijan, but also your future career as a Party leader."

"Can we count on your support?" asked the guest, lowering his voice.

For the first time throughout the conversation, his host looked the man from Baku straight in the eyes, and nodded silently.

The black Volga, with the man from Baku in the back seat, soon sailed through the gates, passed the guard on duty, and swept off again along the Rublyov highway, this time in the opposite direction, to the Domodedovo airport.

Going over in his mind every word the Big Man had spoken, the man from Baku did not notice that the car was being followed, as though attached by an invisible thread to an apparently very ordinary little Moskvich, which had emerged from the road alongside the house. What is more, for some reason the bull-necked driver also paid no attention to the little car, although he must certainly have caught sight of it in his rear-view mirror. He just picked up the car telephone and said something quietly into it. The many policemen on duty along the road looked away immediately when they saw the two cars, both bearing the secret registration numbers of the state security service, the KGB. What the policemen did not know was that both in the KGB and inside the Politburo, two powerful groups were locked in a life-or-death struggle for power. Only one elderly captain of police shook his head in disapproval when the black Volga, followed by the Moskvich, overtook a bus full of people, forcing it to pull onto the curb.

Meanwhile, the listener had realized that the meeting was over. He shut down his equipment, put it under a violin in a case, tossed it down into a pile of snow and started to feel his way down the trunk of the tree.

The attic window of the Big Man's house opened slightly. A gun barrel with optical sights appeared, followed by a quiet *bang*.

The listener dropped like a rag doll. A dark patch of blood spread into the snow from the back of his neck. Three tough young men in track suits hopped quickly over the fence. One of them quickly picked up the violin case, while the other two grabbed the listener by his feet and dragged him into the depths of the fir plantation.

By now, the black Volga had turned off the narrow Rublyov highway onto the orbital road and was speeding along even faster than before, as were the two men in the Moskvich. But at the turn-off for Domodedovo airport, a huge dump-truck suddenly appeared. It let the black Volga pass. The driver of the Moskvich hooted desperately and slammed his foot on the brake. The car skidded and hit the truck head-on, and there it stuck, flattened out like a beer can.

When the traffic police arrived on the scene, all they found was two dead men in the Moskvich, and an empty driver's cab on the truck.

The police quietly set about making their report. It was a very familiar case—just another road accident. The senior policeman bent over to look beneath the truck, where he suddenly caught sight of the registration of the Moskvich, with the revealing "55" of the counter-intelligence service. The expression on his face changed immediately and he rushed to the radio telephone in his patrol car.

General Kramarenko received a report that the Big Man's people had resorted to extreme measures. They had killed two regular officers of the KGB who had been carrying out surveillance duties at a country house on the Rublyov highway.

When that report landed on the desk in his office on Dzerzhinsky Square, Kramarenko realized that fate had opened up for him a long-awaited opportunity. The general had been carrying out the duties of a deputy chairman of the KGB for many years and was one of a group of senior KGB officials who supported the line taken by the new General Secretary. Unlike the old numbskulls in both the Party Central Committee and the KGB, they understood that times had changed and that the Stalinist methods of terror would not be capable of maintaining the Soviet Union in the role of leading Communist state. It needed some liberal, cosmetic treatment to give the Soviet system a more humane image—not out of any high-flown desire to do good to one's fellow beings, but for purely practical reasons.

In the first place, it would persuade world public opinion, deeply shocked by the revelations about the horrors of the Stalin period, to look more favorably on the Soviet Union. If the new policy, both domestic and foreign, succeeded in winning over world opinion, there would be a real possibility of acquiring the Western technology that was so badly needed by the Soviet arms industry. In the second place, by giving Soviet society the external attributes of democracy, it might be possible to inject some life into the Soviet people, utterly exasperated by the eternal shortages of the most elementary goods and housing. The idiots in the ideology department of the Central Committee had understood at last that publishing a couple of dozen books by previously banned authors and stopping the jamming of foreign broadcasts in Russian would not be destroying the Soviet state's foundations.

The general knew very well from the reports provided by his network of informants that the works of Solzhenitsyn were being read and the foreign broadcasts listened to by the same people as had previously, beneath the bedclothes, read forbidden writings and listened to foreign broadcasts. But the great majority of the population were so embittered by the daily struggle for existence that they cared nothing for the unintelligible poems of Brodsky, or for the fate of Doctor Zhivago or of Pasternak. Some softening-up of the regime was essential. The economy demanded it. That was Kramarenko's view. Forced labor at the present level of technology was not productive. A slave could not operate the latest machines.

The pre-industrial Luddite movement of English history was now being repeated in the Soviet Union. Sabotage, both covert and open, was rife—people did not want to work. The country was like a barrel dried out for the summer. It needed some hot water to be poured into it to make it swell up again and stop leaking. But the iron bands around the barrel kept it from bursting apart. (Kramarenko's father had been a village cooper.) In any case, why worry about the Soviet system? The network of atomic power stations scattered across the

Soviet Union now held the whole of mankind hostage. The accident at Chernobyl had make that clear. It would be enough to press the right button in each station for there to be no need for any nuclear war.

But the role of the leader of the Soviet Union in the world was quite another matter. That was what made it necessary to put the country's whole economic system under such a strain in order to keep improving its weapons. It was not books by Solzhenitsyn they had to be afraid of, but the gathering military and economic might of Communist China. That was the country that would become the main problem in the future, not far-off America.

But meanwhile there was a struggle going on in the Party and the KGB, and no one could say who would come out on top. Big Man No. 2 had the backing of practically the whole of the gigantic Party machine, the basic units of which penetrated the vital organs of the state in the boroughs, towns and regions like a network of blood vessels. But the Chairman of the KGB himself, General Kramarenko's immediate boss, was taking a rather indeterminate position. "He's a crafty old boy," his colleagues said of him behind his back. Reticent in his old age, he had been head of personnel administration of the KGB for twenty years, until the day when Andropov, having himself become General Secretary, made him Chairman. The old man retained in his memory not only facts from the secret dossiers relating to his colleagues; he also knew a great deal about every member of the Politburo. He knew about things that had taken place in the lives of many, many people that they tried not to recall even when they were quite alone. Consequently the old man could exert whatever pressure was needed on every member of the Government and Politburo. The old man kept twisting and turning—he wasn't yours and he wasn't ours. But by virtue of the conservative outlook typical to his age, he was more inclined to support the policy of the Big Man who dreamt of being General Secretary.

The Big Man was trying to rock the throne of the young General Secretary by inciting pogroms in Azerbaijan and unrest in Armenia. He wanted to depict the leader to everyone as weak, incapable of governing a multinational country like the Soviet Union. The increasingly frequent comments in the national newspapers about rising crime rates were also the Big Man's work. He was out to frighten the population. He wanted people to start longing again for the days of Stalin, for public order and the firm hand, when—however frightful it was to be alive—you could stroll around the city at night without fear of being mugged or raped.

Well, a little pogrom might act as a good shock for the Armenians who were shouting too much about their independence. Let them learn the hard way, the general thought to himself, that they won't find it easy without us.

Today Kramarenko had obtained the chance he needed to help the General Secretary. He would help him to bring down the Big Man—and at the same time remove his own boss from his position as Chairman. Then they would see.

TWO

Kramarenko summoned his best operative, Major Simonov, and ordered him to set up a special group to investigate the deaths of two officers in a car accident.

"On top of that, check the lists of all passengers arriving at Domodedovo airport. You may come across a familiar name. And, Lyosha"—the general remembered something and noisily cracked his finger joints, a habit for which his wife was always reproaching him—"I want to talk to the driver of the car that delivered the unknown man to the airport."

The name of the driver of the black Volga was Kamayev, Senior Lieutenant of State Security Victor Kamayev.

Having delivered the man from Baku to the airport and taken him right up to the steps into the plane, Kamayev had decided to earn a little money on the side. With the keys of the car dangling from his hand, he passed along the long line-up at the taxi stand. "To the city center. . . . Who wants the center?" he said quietly.

"How much do you charge?" inquired two old ladies, who had just arrived with suitcases and bags crammed full of presents for their Moscow relations.

"Depends where you want to go," Kamayev said in a business-like tone.

One of them delved into her bosom and pulled out a scrap of paper with the address. "To Tyoply Stan, that's it," she said.

"Twenty rubles."

The women gasped in unison.

"It's only a few rubles more than by taxi," Kamayev explained, and added, "That's because it's quicker and more comfortable."

The two women whispered to each other and then agreed. An icy wind was sweeping across the square in front of the airport, and they couldn't see the end of the line-up for taxis. "Moscow is Moscow," they said with a sigh. "Take us, please."

After dropping off the old ladies, Kamayev drove on to a little shop he knew of, in a new district of Moscow, where the line for vodka was always shorter than in the center of town. Downtown, especially towards the end of the working day, there were always mile-long lines at the liquor shops, as well as violent quarrels and fights.

This time, though, Kamayev was out of luck. There already were some 300 men, many driven wild by their hangovers, swarming around the shop door, and two squads of police were having trouble holding back the crowd struggling to get to the counter.

Kamayev locked the car and slipped through a back door to the office of the shop manager. There he presented a phony certificate confirming the death of his father. Such official documents were issued specially, and stamped by undertakers, to enable people to buy spirits in large quantities for funerals and weddings. An ordinary customer who did not possess such a document was allowed to buy only one bottle of vodka and one bottle of wine. If he needed more, he had to wait in line all over again. That was how the authorities fought alcoholism and the black market in strong drink.

The manager was about to start swearing at his visitor about joining the people who had lined up in the usual way, when he saw the otter-skin hat Kamayev was wearing and realized at once what organization his visitor was from. He went himself to fetch five bottles of Stolichnaya vodka.

No sooner had Kamayev put the bottles in the trunk of the car than a man with a crafty look in his eyes approached him.

"Take me to the three main railway stations, chief," he said.

Kamayev looked him over slowly, and opened the door of the

Volga. "Ten rubles, and cash up front," he warned the little man, who had already dived into the car.

"You don't trust me?"

Kamayev muttered something indistinct, and made it clear that the car was not going anywhere until the man handed over the fare, swearing under his breath.

All the way down Trade Union Street, the man kept questioning Kamayev, to find out who Kamayev's boss was to have such a luxurious Volga, complete with telephone. But Kamayev concentrated on his driving and kept silent.

"Which station do you want?" he asked when they had joined the Garden Ring.

"The Kazan station, that's the one," the man said. "I'm catching a train to Orenburg. Listen, pal," he said, dropping his voice, "I've got a long way to go, and a boring trip. I'd like to get my hands on a bottle of vodka, but you saw what a line there was. And I was afraid of missing my train. You wouldn't help me out, would you?"

"How many do you want?"

"Two bottles."

"Thirty rubles."

"It's a deal!" said the man, seemingly pleased. "Just the thing to make my journey shorter."

At Lermontov Square, the Volga swung around in the direction of the Kazan station. "Drive in there," said the man, pointing to a passageway that led to the luggage office. "I'll just stop in and get my case to hide the vodka. Will you wait?"

"I'll wait," Kamayev grunted.

The man disappeared into the crowd, while Kamayev got out of the car to stretch his legs.

The Kazan station was swarming with people. It seemed as though the whole country were on the move in one direction or the other: whole families were sleeping on their luggage, waiting for a train; soldiers were wandering aimlessly around, their trenchcoats unbuttoned; men on official trips carrying heavy briefcases strode purposefully through the crowd; and the Tatar porters with their carts shouted to each other.

"Here I am," said the man as he emerged from the crowd. "Give me the booze, brother." He opened the case to receive the bottles.

Kamayev opened the trunk of the car and lifted out the pack with the bottles. At that very moment, a policeman with the rank of captain came up behind them.

"Doing a bit of black market business, are we?" he said with a happy smile, as he laid his hand on the bottles of vodka.

The little man was also smiling. There was a happy glint in his eyes.

"A damned informer," Kamayev said at once to himself. The police used special provocateurs like that in their campaign against the illegal trade in liquor.

"Our posh driver charges his customers very reasonable prices, Sergei," the man informed the captain. "No more than fifteen rubles a bottle."

Kamayev pushed the captain's hand off the packet, put the vodka back in the car trunk, and closed it.

"You're wasting your time, mister," the captain said calmly. "Even though you're driving a KGB car, you'll still be in trouble for black marketeering." The police disliked people who worked in the KGB because of the privileges they enjoyed. Kamayev took out a red certificate and held it close to the captain's face. It bore a red stamp, and said that the Volga car with this particular number was not subject to being stopped or inspected by the police.

The captain's face dropped at once.

"You despicable little twerp," Kamayev spat at the pathetic man. "And you, captain," added the senior lieutenant of state security as he opened the car door, "You are a secondhand French letter."

Major Simonov succeeded in tracking Kamayev down that same evening. He put out a message to all the police on duty along the Rublyov highway, and it proved quite easy to pick up the driver of the black Volga. The major instructed Kamayev to return the car to its official garage and go to a subway station. There, he was hustled into a waiting car, exactly the same kind of black Volga with radio equipment sticking up as Kamayev had been driving around all day.

People returning from work saw Kamayev being seized, and got out of the way. No one came to his aid. On the other hand, Kamayev, a strong and very fit man, put up a furious resistance, with the result that he had to be injected with a sedative.

The KGB's safe house was situated in the center of the city on Vorovsky street, next to Vspolny lane. Operatives belonging to the special group picked up Kamayev, still prostrate after the injection, and carried him into the entrance. The elevator was not working, of course, so they had to carry the man up to the fifth floor. "Taken a drop too much," said an old woman they met on the stairs. "What silly people you are; what on earth are you doing to yourselves?"

The apartment they dragged Kamayev into had a special room without windows. The floor, the walls and the ceiling of that room were all covered in gray wallpaper over a thick layer of rubber, sufficient to deaden any sound. In the center of the room there was a wooden armchair with an upright back. It was screwed to the floor and had clamps to hold the arms and legs. There were also two powerful lights aimed at the chair. To one side there was an ordinary office desk and chair.

They stripped Kamayev, even removing his underwear, and sat him naked in the chair, put the clamps on his arms and legs and gave him another injection. The major lit a cigarette, sat on the edge of his desk and waited for the injection to take effect.

Kamayev's eyes were open, but the pupils were moving around uncontrollably. Gradually, they began to settle down to a normal expression. Simonov switched on the directional lights, and a dazzling beam lit up the room and Kamayev's face. The major himself remained in the semi-darkness.

Kamayev came around at last, and when he did he let out a mighty growl and tried to burst out of the chair. But the automatic clamps only gripped his arms more tightly.

"Take it easy, Kamayev," said the major. "You'd be better off telling me who it was you drove out to Domodedovo today."

Kamayev understood very well the sort of hole he was in. More than once he had driven all sorts of people to similar rooms in safe houses, had helped to undress them, so that they would be overcome by a feeling of childlike helplessness, and had even been present at the interrogation. Kamayev was well aware of something else, too—that if he opened his mouth, his life would come to an end in a few days. He would be tracked down by the people he worked for and who worked for the Big Man. But it was more likely that these people would put an end to him in any case—once they had squeezed what they needed out of him. Then they would cart him off at night to the city dump, having already mutilated his face and cut off the tips of his fingers. Then they would throw his naked body to the rats for supper. After that his own mother would not recognize him, let alone a police investigator.

"I'm waiting, Kamayev."

Kamayev turned the situation over feverishly in his head. "It all depends on how they are going to beat me up," he thought. "If they give me the whole treatment that'll mean I'm headed for the dump. But if they do it without leaving any marks, and I hold out, they will try to recruit me to their side and make me into an informer in the Big Man's crowd."

"Well, you're the boss," said the major, standing up. "We didn't want to hurt you, but it looks as if we shall have to."

A couple of operatives came into the room, sealed Kamayev's mouth with plaster and set about giving him a brutal beating. Kamayev simply groaned from the pain without being able to make out just how they were beating him—doing him actual bodily harm, or simply hitting him around the kidneys and heart.

The telephone rang in the next room. The operatives stopped what they were doing and, breathing heavily, looked at Simonov.

"Carry on," he said with a nod and went into the next room.

It was General Kramarenko on the line. "How's it going?" he asked.

"He still won't talk."

"Alyosha,"—the general spelled it out clearly—"I need to know who he drove to the airport." And he put down the receiver.

The major got the message. He went back into the padded room, sent the operatives out of the room, and took off his jacket.

What he then did to Kamayev no one knew. But half an hour later Simonov came out of the room dripping with sweat and with a strange expression on his face. With shaking hands he took the cigarette offered him, inhaled deeply a few times and then picked up the telephone.

"Comrade General," he said, "I am ready to report to you."

THREE

Due to a strange combination of circumstances, Gerald Jacobson, an American journalist and Moscow correspondent of the Star newspaper, found himself in Yerevan, capital of Armenia.

His editor had instructed him to write a series of travel notes about the beauties of that mountainous country, and his request for permission to make the trip had been supported by the all-powerful "Intourist" organization. The Soviet travel industry was interested in the publication of such material, believing that it would attract tourists from the United States. The Soviet Ministry of Foreign Affairs had been fairly quick in issuing him with the necessary visa, but unfortunately, he had caught a bad cold and was shut up for a couple of weeks in his office, a two-roomed apartment on Kutuzov avenue in Moscow. By the time he was fit again, it was the beginning of February and there was trouble in Nagorno-Karabakh and Yerevan. The Soviet authorities immediately banned all travel to Armenia and Azerbaijan.

Like every good newspaper man, Gerald Jacobson was always inclined to take a chance. His visa was still valid, and he decided to try to get into the closed city of Yerevan, rightly counting on the usual bureaucratic confusion reigning throughout the Soviet administrative system. So he set off for the Ukraina hotel, in whose huge lobby Aeroflot had an office that served only foreigners.

A pretty girl in a blue Aeroflot uniform checked his permit to travel, and without any further questions she issued Gerald a ticket. She handed it to him in his passport, and with a pleasant smile wished him a safe journey.

It was still daylight when his plane landed at Yerevan's Zvartnots airport, which was famous not only for its original architecture but also for having been the scene of the first bloody battles fought by Russian special forces, pumped full of drugs, against Armenian demonstrators.

Gerald was met by two young people in fashionable coats representing the local branch of Intourist—a Russian by the name of Vasili, and an Armenian known as Hamlet. (Gerald was later to come across a Laertes and even a Juliet—for some reason or other the Armenians liked to give their children names from Shakespeare.) The two young men were to accompany Gerald on his trip around the republic, according to an itinerary already agreed on in Moscow. It came as something of a surprise to Gerald that these two charming young people recognized him immediately among the great crowd of passengers arriving from Moscow. He concluded at once that Intourist was not the only organization they worked for, despite their apparently frank smiles. It was Gerald's second year working in the Soviet Union and he knew very well that practically all Russians who regularly came into contact with foreigners were connected one way or another with the KGB. It was the only institution in that country that still operated efficiently.

The young men from Intourist put Gerald into a car and took him to his hotel, treating him on the way to the latest mildly anti-Soviet witticisms, involving questions to "Yerevan radio." At the hotel, he was provided with a luxurious room looking out over a beautiful fountain—but from then on "everything in the Oblonsky house got very confused," as Tolstoy had remarked in a novel Gerald had read when he was young.

The hard drinking started on the very first day, when they took him to the mountain lake of Sevan. They lit a fire on the shores of the lake and roasted *shashlyk* that gave off a marvelous smell of sizzling meat. A white tablecloth was laid out on the ground, and covered with tomatoes still warm from the sun, green cucumbers, radishes, heaps of tender freshly picked Armenian salad, and pieces of white sheep's cheese. Among all this magnificence stood the long necks of the elegant bottles of Armenian brandy, surrounded by chilled bottles of Borzhom and Narzan mineral water, looking like faithful servants of the brandy. And in the distance, rising above the smooth blue surface of the lake, could be seen the dazzling white summit of Mount Ararat.

Through every day that followed, Gerald had the feeling that he was floating in a pink mist—a trip along the twisting mountain roads to the little health spa of Dilizhan, then to the remarkable church at Gerat, and to the modest, dignified churches in Echmiadzin . . . and all this interwoven with meals in restaurants where Gerald danced Armenian national dances to the accompaniment of Armenian instruments, and visits to hospitable homes where he was expected to drink wine out of huge antique silver horns. Poor Gerald's head, befuddled by drink, was ringing on the one hand with noisy formal toasts in his honor and on the other with the whisperings of Hamlet and Vasili, each of whom, in an effort to inspire him with confidence, told him that the other was a police informer and urged him to be cautious. Although the drink made it difficult for him to think clearly, Gerald realized why he was being put through such a program of nonstop entertainment. He was not supposed to see what was taking place in this town. He had to be kept away from the meetings at the Opera House attended by hundreds of thousands of people, from the demonstrations, the tanks on the streets, the armed patrols, and a lot of other things that the Soviet government hoped to conceal from the rest of the world.

In his rare solitary moments, when he woke up in the morning and find himself half-undressed on the bed in his hotel room, Gerald would ask himself in hung-over depression whether he would ever be able to write what was expected of him—whether in fact he would ever write another line for the rest of his life. But every time he found himself in this state, Hamlet and Vasili, freshly shaven and full of life, would appear at the door of his room. Without giving their suffering guest time for his mental torture to develop into a state of manic depression, they would immediately pour him half a glass of brandy, and the whole routine would start over again.

A full week went by in this drunken way, until the day when Gerald woke up and realized that he'd had enough. If he didn't wish to meet his end far from his native land, he would have to call a halt to the drinking. One more glass and his soul, along with his body, would be carried up to heaven. He was in a state comparable with that of a dog run over by a car.

Only with difficulty could Gerald unstick his eyelids. He could see a pale, early-morning sky through the half-closed shutters of the windows. "I must get some oxygen into my blood—maybe that will help," Gerald said to himself, and decided to go outside and take a walk before his murderously hospitable hosts put in an appearance.

Gerald got up, rather unsteady on his feet, overcame the desire to collapse back into the bed, and staggered into the bathroom, trying not to catch sight of his swollen face. He didn't dare to brush his teeth—the very thought of doing so made him feel like retching. When he swore about it, he couldn't recognize his own voice, it was so hoarse.

Having cleaned himself up, he felt a little more confident. His mind slowly became clearer, and objects in the room began to assume their real outlines. So he then dressed himself, the effort still causing him to sweat profusely, and made his way out of the hotel.

Outside, the wind was blowing paper and trash around the deserted square. The fountain was not working. A yellow traffic light was flashing on and off at an intersection, and there was not a soul to be seen, with the exception of a policeman on duty protecting a huge monument to Lenin. (Because of the events in Nagorno-Karabakh, someone had tried to disfigure it recently and the authorities had therefore put a guard on it.)

Shivering from the cold, Gerald strolled through the sleeping city, without any clear purpose. He had traveled the whole world, but Yerevan evoked mixed feelings in Gerald. He was put off by the unconcealed poverty of the old, primitive dwellings that could be seen even in the center of the city, but, strangely enough, he liked the national architectural style, in which the modern buildings had been built from tufa. At first glance this deep-pink rock from the mountains gave the houses a rather gloomy and ponderous look, but once you got used to it you felt the warmth given off by the tufa. It was as if the stone were giving off the heat it had absorbed from the hot sun of Armenia. This feeling in turn evoked a response—it seemed as though you were the guest of a good host.

Without realizing it, Gerald reached the square dominated by the

Opera. He had already been shown this beautiful building as he was being driven through the square, but his guides had stubbornly insisted for various reasons on postponing his visit to it. Gerald had heard that it was the place where the people of Yerevan gathered for the meetings in defense of Nagorno-Karabakh, but he had not pressed very strongly to inspect it. His main preoccupation at the time had been not to accidentally set off the explosive mixture of brandy, various kinds of wine and unbelievably strong grape vodka that had been poured into him.

In front of the theater entrance there were two statues of some learned men whose difficult Armenian names Gerald could not decipher. Up against the marble base of one of these, huddled in a light blanket, a young girl was dozing. There were flowers scattered around her feet, and higher up, there was a sign stuck to the plinth of the statue, handwritten in Armenian script. Gerald approached the girl. Hearing the footsteps of a person approaching on the asphalt, the girl opened her eyes, revealing her long eyelashes.

Gerald stopped. The girl's dark eyes expressed such genuine grief that he felt a lump in his throat. "What's happened?" Gerald muttered in English. He wasn't able to read the sign. "What are you doing here?"

The girl did not reply.

"Can I be of any help?"

The girl hung her little head, wrapped in a black scarf. Gerald repeated his question in his broken Russian. A tear trickled down the girl's cheek.

Gerald didn't know what to do. "Perhaps you need some money?" The thought suddenly occurred to him, and he reached for his wallet. "Here you are!" He pulled out all the money he had with him, Russian rubles, American dollars and English pounds, and placed it on the girl's lap. "Do me a favor—take it."

She remained as silent as before.

The sky was becoming ever lighter, and the purple reflection of the rising sun rose behind the mountains. The birds in the tops of the trees came to life, beginning to sing and flutter around in the foliage. There was a light wind blowing, which swept the money from the girl's lap. But she simply went on watching indifferently as the colored notes were scattered around the square.

Somewhat embarrassed, Gerald bent down and started to pick
them up. Suddenly he felt somebody's powerful hands grabbing
ahold of him, and he found himself face to face with a tough and
very angry young man in a leather jacket. He had not noticed him
coming out of the side street.

"Who do you think you're forcing money on, you jackass?" he
shouted in Russian, with a terrible accent. Because of Gerald's fair
hair and blue eyes, the young man had mistaken him for a Russian.

"I only wanted to help—I had no bad intentions . . . " Gerald
began to explain, in an even stronger accent than the young man's.
This made the man even angrier, and he grabbed Gerald by the
lapels and shook him.

"You trying to copy me?"

In a mixture of English and Russian, Gerald managed to convey
to the young man that he was an American journalist and that he
had no improper thoughts regarding the girl. The misunderstanding
was cleared up. Levon, as the young man was called, told Gerald
about himself and about the girl sitting at the monument. He spoke
quite tolerable English, though with the same strong accent. It
turned out that both he and the girl were students at Yerevan University, in the philosophy department.

"I am helping Arpik to maintain her hunger strike, and I act as
her guard," Levon said. "The Azerbaijanis in Nagorno-Karabakh
murdered her parents and she has gone on hunger strike as a protest.
It's the fourth day she hasn't eaten—she demands that the authorities
punish the murders."

As he told the story, Levon was gently massaging the girl's frozen
back. The blanket slipped off her thin shoulders, allowing Gerald to
see two photographs pinned to her knitted pullover. One showed a
middle-aged man and a woman who looked like Arpik. They were
staring into the camera with serious expressions. The other, in black
and white, showed two practically naked corpses lying against a
brick wall. With a shudder Gerald realized that both photos were of
the girl's murdered parents.

"You poor girl," he said in a half-whisper, and again felt the lump
rising in his throat. The girl looked at him and then buried her face
in Levon's chest.

"I knew nothing about this," said Gerald. "The Soviet newspapers and television assert that, apart from the strikes in Nagorno-Karabakh and the meetings in Yerevan, nothing terrible has taken place in the Caucasus."

"Of course nothing is taking place," said Levon bitterly. "So a few Armenians perished. Do you think that's likely to make anybody's heart beat faster in Moscow?"

They both remained silent.

"If it wasn't for Vozgen being there," Levon cried out suddenly with real fire, "we would have shed some of their blood too!"

"What's the Catholicos got to do with it?" Gerald asked in some surprise. Like most of the foreign journalists in Moscow, in February he'd had no clear idea of what was really taking place in Armenia and Azerbaijan. They'd had to make do with rumors they could not verify, and had no means of knowing where the truth lay.

"There are now a hundred and sixty thousand Azerbaijanis living in Armenia," Levon explained. "When force was first used against the Armenian population in Nagorno-Karabakh, the Catholicos Vozgen, head of the Grigorian church of Armenia, appeared on Yerevan television and said, 'If any Armenian sheds the blood of Azerbaijanis he will curse the day he was born and will be silent forever.' And Vozgen is the only person whom we Armenians trust and respect."

"He is probably right," Gerald commented hesitantly. "Hatred generates only more hatred and bloodshed provokes more bloodshed."

"We understand that, and that's why we don't want to be judged by the same standards as these Azerbaijanis have. Or, to be precise, as those among them who took to their knives."

"Listen, Levon," said Gerald. "The Soviet authorities do everything they can to prevent we Western journalists in Moscow from obtaining reliable information. They don't give us the possibility of digging down to the truth. Tell me what is really going on in Armenia and Azerbaijan—and try to be objective."

"Just wait a moment . . . "

Levon gave the girl a drink of hot tea from a thermos flask, wrapped her up again in the blanket and then took Gerald to one side where there was a little shop on the corner of a side street.

"Let Arpik sleep so long as there are no people about," he said tenderly, nodding in the direction of the sad little figure lying against the base of the marble monument.

"I shall write about her," Gerald promised.

"Arpik doesn't need to be made famous. What she wants is that such a loss as she has suffered should never befall anybody else." Levon remained silent for a while, and then continued. "The essence of the conflict is this: The authorities in Azerbaijan are gradually but insistently forcing the Armenian population out of Nagorno-Karabakh. It is, incidentally, a very fertile region and it used to belong to Armenia. And this is not the only such case."

Gerald pulled out a notebook and began with a rather shaky hand to record what young Levon was telling him.

He learned that such regions now forming part of Azerbaijan as Nakhichevan (a name that, literally translated, means "the place where God has trodden"), Nagorno-Karabakh and other Armenian lands were annexed by force to Moslem Azerbaijan at the demand of Turkey in the 1920s. Lenin, then taken up with saving the Soviet regime in Russia itself, easily agreed to hand these regions over. Anything to prevent yet another military conflict in a country torn apart by civil war. The cunning Turks had made skillful use of a favorable situation and had nothing to lose. The historic aim of Turkey's foreign policy at that time, as in the case of the Ayatollah Khomeini in the 1980s, consisted in the outward expansion of Moslem influence: to bring all the peoples of the Caucasus and Trans-Caucasus under the domination of Islam. A secret instruction written by the Minister of War in the Turkish government has been preserved. It says straightforwardly: "Armenia and the Armenian people, being a people professing the teaching of Christ, must be completely annihilated." This decree did not remain just paper—it was a guide to action. In 1915, Turks butchered a million and a half Armenians and seized all the best lands in the Ararat valley, which remains to this day in the hands of the Turks. It was a huge genocide. The Azerbaijanis are now trying by semilegal methods to obtain the regions that the Turks did not then succeed in annexing. Although Azerbaijan, like Armenia, is considered to be Soviet, the people there are obviously drawn to Iran and Turkey, inhabited by people of the same Moslem faith.

"So what does the present Soviet government have to answer for?" Gerald inquired. "Why have they taken up such an ambiguous position, backing neither one side or the other? Logically Moscow ought to support the just demands of the people living in Nagorno-

Karabakh, not play into the hands of the Moslem chauvinists."

Levon laughed. "'There are more things in heaven and earth, Horatio, than are dreamt of in your philosophy,'" he quoted from Shakespeare. "Only I would rephrase it—'There are more things in Soviet life, Mister Jacobson—'"

"Just call me Gerald."

"Do you honestly want to know what is now going on in Nagorno-Karabakh, and why Moscow has adopted such a position?"

"I'm a newsman, Levon."

"And you're not afraid?"

"In this life I'm only afraid of catching VD," Gerald joked, adding after a moment's thought, "And of hangovers, I suppose."

"You're a lucky guy," Levon said enviously. "If you'd been born in the Soviet Union, you would have regarded VD as no more than a common cold, and a hangover would be guaranteed every morning."

"I gather you have an idea?"

"I have a friend who has her own car and speaks excellent English. If, Gerald, you were ready to take a chance, the three of us could spend a day in Stepanokert. It's the capital of Nagorno-Karabakh, and that's where the main events are now taking place."

Gerald said nothing, reflecting on what was a very tempting proposal.

"It's very important for us Armenians that people in the West should know the truth. Moreover, it should be written, not by an Armenian, an Azerbaijani or a Russian, but objectively by an American. Do you agree?"

Gerald had the feeling that the tight bands that had been gripping his head were slackening off, and he was beginning to take an interest in what was going on around him. Levon was a very pleasant young man, and his idea promised to result in a really sensational story. To write a series of reports from Nagorno-Karabakh, which was closed to all foreign newsmen, and to have photographs to accompany it. . . . That wouldn't be the travel guide to the beauties of Armenia that his editor had asked for. It would be front-page news! His father, an old and experienced newspaper man, had been right when he had said, "If good luck passes you by, just hang around!" It looked now as if his lucky moment had come. After all, what was he risking by making such a trip without official permission from the authorities? An unpleasant encounter when they discovered that he had violated the ban? They might force him to go back to Moscow or, at the worst, expel him from the country. But he would have done a good job, and Gerald was already pretty fed up with life in the Soviet Union. It was a fiendishly boring life, in which even the women he got to know were planted on him by the KGB. Most important, he would get his hands on rich material that would enable him to make a big name for himself.

"Have you made up your mind?" asked Levon with a penetrating look, trying to read the expression on Gerald's face.

"Yes, I have," said Gerald. "Only it will be a tricky business getting rid of the Intourist people who are looking after me. They are by no means stupid.

"So listen," he finally said, decisively. "Wait for me tomorrow at seven in the morning in the square around the corner from the hotel."

"By the thousand fountains?" asked Levon to be sure.

"Yes, I think that's what they call it." Gerald had been in the square and remembered the long line of rather strikingly designed fountains which played along the whole length of the main avenue.

"How are you going to get rid of your informers?"

"That's my problem," said Gerald, regaining some of his usual self-confidence. "Don't you worry."

"You're a good fellow, Gerald," said Levon with real feeling, as he stood up. "You will be doing a good deed, not just for my people, but for others too. Remember the immortal words of John Donne— 'Do not ask for whom the bell tolls. It tolls for you.'"

Gerald regarded these last words from Levon as rather over-emotional, but made allowances for his youth, and the fact that he was studying philosophy.

The sun had already risen and was shining through the windows of the hotel when he got back to the room, where he found a very worried Hamlet and Vasili hanging around his door.

"Where did you get to, Gerald?" They rushed towards him with evident relief.

Gerald said meaningfully that he had been seeing a beautiful girl home. With a glance at the incredulous expressions on the faces of his faithful companions, he made for the bathroom to wash and shave.

That day, despite all efforts to persuade him, Gerald did not take a single drink. He spent a long time strolling around the quiet Metandaran, the specially built museum housing the most ancient Armenian manuscripts, and in the evening he said he was too tired to go out to a restaurant and went back to his hotel. There, politely but firmly, he showed the disappointed Hamlet and Vasili the door.

Even so they didn't leave him alone. Throughout the evening the telephone kept ringing in the hotel room. When Gerald took up the phone there would be various voices, sometimes a man's, sometimes a woman's, apologizing for the mistake and hanging up. Gerald realized that they were checking to see whether he was in the hotel or had gone out. The ringing continued until late in the evening when Gerald decided he had had enough. He took the phone off the hook and left it lying on the table. He then collapsed into bed, having set his alarm clock for six o'clock in the morning.

Gerald awoke before the alarm went off. For the first time since the day he had arrived in Yerevan he had had a good sleep and felt himself to be in good form. Without switching on the light in his room, so that it should not be seen from the street, Gerald quickly gathered his things together and wrote a note to his "friends" in which he told them teasingly that he was taking a couple of days off. He wanted to spend those days with a beautiful woman and begged Hamlet and Vasili not to worry about him. When his amorous passion had subsided, he would turn up again at the hotel himself. Gerald knew very well that his young friends and the professional KGB men in the background were unlikely to be taken in by such a simple trick. But to hell with them! The rules of the game had been observed.

Gerald checked once again to make sure he had his documents and his wallet, hooked his trusty Nikon camera with its telephoto lens over his shoulder, and stepped out onto the balcony.

From that height, he could see clearly the whole of the deserted square, still lit by the street lamps, as well as the part of the square where the others were to wait for him. In daytime he had taken note of the scaffolding surrounding the eastern facade, where workmen were changing the rendering on the building. There was a decorative ledge leading to the scaffolding, and Gerald hoped to use it to reach the scaffolding and then make his way to the ground. In theory it wasn't a very difficult descent. The ledge encircling the whole building was wide enough, although it sloped towards the street. Now came the moment to take the first step over the five-story drop.

"Okay," Gerald said to himself, "if you've sat down at the table and picked up the cards, you'd better play." And, stuffing the folds of his long raincoat into his belt to keep from tripping on them, Gerald stepped over the railing of the balcony and edged his way along cautiously, pressing his body tightly against the rough wall.

He managed to get past the neighboring balcony and another barrier, and found himself at the faintly lit window that looked into the corridor where the woman on duty was sitting. All the Soviet hotels in which Gerald had been accommodated had had similar duty women on each floor. Their function was a strange one. They didn't clean the rooms, they didn't change the bedclothes, and the keys to the rooms were handed in to the reception in the hall. The women simply sat there the whole day long, each on her own floor, watching to see that none of the guests took a woman into his room. In this connection the Soviet authorities were mercilessly puritanical, as indeed they were in everything else that concerned the private life of the people.

On this occasion the duty woman was not in her place, but Hamlet and Vasili were dozing in the armchairs next to her desk. They were making sure he didn't dodge them again. "You'll be in trouble tomorrow," Gerald thought maliciously, "when the KGB gets to know about my disappearance."

At that moment Vasili opened his eyes and stretched himself.

Gerald froze still. If Vasili were to raise his eyes now, he would see Gerald framed in the window—an American journalist hanging onto the window from the outside. But Vasili only glanced at his watch, stretched out his long legs into a more comfortable position and dozed off again.

So as to slip past the dangerous window as quickly as possible Gerald speeded up his movements, took an uncertain step and nearly lost his footing completely. Suddenly dripping with sweat, he pressed himself against the wall again and remained stock still. He stayed like that for some time to give his wildly beating heart the chance to calm down and only then, taking great precautions, did he move towards the scaffolding.

Levon was already waiting for him in the square near the fountains. He was genuinely delighted to see Gerald and shook him firmly by the hand. "To tell you the truth," he admitted as they strode towards the car, which as a precaution had been left in the next street. "I doubted whether you would turn up."

"And you were right to do so," said Gerald. He was still trembling because of the fright he had given himself. "It is better to think worse about people than they really are. Then it's all the nicer to find out the truth."

Gerald was pleasantly surprised. Levon's friend turned out to be an athletic-looking girl in pants and a tight sweater. Gerald was even more impressed by her wonderful gray eyes, rarely seen in Armenian women.

"Sevda," she said, introducing herself briefly, and took the wheel.

"With such a driver," Gerald informed Levon, "I'm ready to drive to New Zealand, to the Land of Fire!"

"Karabakh is today also aflame, a country on fire," said the girl drawing her dark eyebrows into a frown. "And not in the figurative sense, but literally." And with that she made the car accelerate violently.

Relaxing in the soft seat of the Lada, Gerald congratulated himself on having decided to make the trip. A pretty girl, the foretaste of danger—it all tended to make the blood run faster. He could already imagine himself in America among his friends, sitting at an open fireplace with a glass of whiskey in his hand and telling the story of his adventure in the distant mountains of the mysterious Caucasus.

FOUR

That February day in Sumgait began more or less as usual. Only the unusually large police units at the entrance to the bank, the city committee and other Party and government institutions indicated that the situation was not entirely normal. Actually there were rather more young people to be seen on the streets, swarming into the central square, and among them were some unshaven characters, obviously criminal types, bobbing in and out.

But in the southern outskirts of Sumgait, where old Aramais lived there was none of this. Down there the day began as usual. The garbage truck came rattling along the cobblestone roadway at the usual time. It was followed by an elderly Tatar, his face wrinkled like a ripe apricot, who kept crying out in a melancholy tone, "I'll buy your old things . . . "

Closer to lunch time, a bright young Russian by the name of Senya appeared on the scene. He set up his knife-grinding bench, took his leather apron out of a canvas bag, spat contemptuously, and cried out in a squeaky boyish voice, "Knives to grind? Scissors to mend?"

The next minute he was surrounded by women with knives and scissors and by grubby street-boys. They all stood there fascinated, watching the sparks streaming from the knives as they met the spinning wheel. In that muddy little side street, with its houses toppling from age, the people were very fond of just staring at something.

The old Azerbaijani women in their long somber dresses and their equally somber headscarves, with wisps of gray hair peeking out, would sit all day long at the entrance to the courtyard. They looked like big black birds, and they followed every movement of the few strangers passing that way. Especially if it was a neighbor accompanied by a woman they didn't know, or a group of tipsy friends.

The most important of the women was old Zeinab, who would sit at the gateway selling hot chestnuts and persimmon from her garden. She knew everything about everybody, so when the women fell to arguing about who was living with whom, she always had the last word. Behind Zeinab's back, the other women would whisper that old Aramais sometimes visited her at night. Aramais's workshop was in a little green-painted hut, with a board on the door that read:

BOOTS AND SHOES REPAIRED
(and sandals)

The hut was right on the corner, next to the half-ruined building of the old school—a favorite place for all the boys on the street. On the second floor practically a whole classroom had survived, along with the blackboard. Someone had written on it in chalk with huge letters, "Hurrah! No lessons—we'll go and beat up the Armenians!" It was there, where a little tree was growing out of a crack in the wall and it smelled of dried manure, that the local lads, sometimes along with old Aramais's son Arshik, sipped wine for the first time, learned to smoke, and hid their homemade knives with fancy, colored handles made from perspex.

And in the cellar beneath the old school there was an auto tire store, and about a hundred feet away from it there was a noisy bar—a little green-painted shop surrounded by empty barrels. There, the barmaid Farida worked wonders with beer. She was a loud-mouthed woman with plucked eyebrows and a crudely made-up face, from which her ever-suspicious eyes looked out as if from a machine gun-post.

Even on normal days there was always a crowd standing around the bar, but that February 27, a Saturday, it was quite impossible to squeeze your way through to the window where Farida was drawing the beer by hand from the barrel.

The patrons were mostly workers who lived in the houses near-by—unshaven men with shoulders sagging from exhaustion. For them the bar was a breath of fresh air, a vent to which they turned after a whole week of hard work in the oil fields of Sumgait. It was a place where they could relax, and escape for an hour or so from their homes, from the everlasting complaints of their wives and their snotty-nosed children, to argue about the latest soccer match or simply to smoke in silence while sipping at a jar of Farida's diluted beer.

The bar also had its regular customers—the complete drop-outs, with their faces puffed out from uncontrolled drinking and their shaking hands. They hung around the bar from the moment it opened and dealt in anything that came along, so long as they could scrap together enough for a bottle of cheap wine, known as "bormo-tukha." Some of them collected empty vodka bottles and changed them into money at the nearest shop. Others simply poured the dregs of beer from other people's mugs into their own tins and made do with that.

One character who hung around the bar was known as "the Goat"—an invalid, well-known in the district, who had lost his left arm and right leg in the war. He would spend his meager pension on drink in a couple of days, but since the Goat's insides were always burning for more and he had no means of buying it, he had found a rather original way of curing his hangover. He would pick on some fortunate possessor of a mug or two of beer who, holding his mugs high above people's heads, would break out of the crowd near the bar and find a place near an empty barrel. The Goat would stagger across on his one crutch and suddenly spit into one of the mugs, which meant of course that no one would drink from it. He usually chose someone with two mugs. If he dared to spit into a person's only mug he might get himself killed. The Goat got beaten up for his tricks, but the mug he had managed to spit into went to him as a reward.

So now, as Shamanidi dropped into the bar, the Goat was being trampled underfoot by a man in cheap canvas boots. "Please don't kill me!" the Goat howled, rolling on the ground. "I must get a drink!" The man just went on kicking him in silence, with occasional outbursts of ferocity, and no one came to the Goat's defense. Farida was in fact already closing her little shop, and the nearest bar was a long way away, and it was by no means certain that the other bar would have any beer. The Goat had not taken this into account, and he was now paying for it.

"You're hurting me!" the invalid continued to shout his protests.

From one of the more distant barrels someone said quietly, "You've had your fun, that's enough now."

It was Maksud speaking. Along with his inseparable companion, the powerful lad Khobot, he was drinking vodka and had set out in front of him a carefully sliced sausage and radish.

The man didn't hear Maksud. He was still kicking the Goat just as vigorously, trying to kick him right in the stomach. Maksud put his half-empty mug down on a barrel, wiped his lips thoughtfully with the end of his white scarf and went up to the man. "Who do you think I was talking to?"

The man looked up, his face red and angry. The people standing around fell silent, curious to see what would happen.

"Bugger off, you swine."

"Who do you think you are?" the man said aggressively.

"Do I have to tell you again?" Maksud's eyes narrowed.

"Who the hell . . . " the man muttered, rather less sure of himself, as he stepped back.

"Get out of here before I poke your eyes out." Maksud was known as a thief throughout the southern part of Sumgait. Muttering curses to himself, the man moved away.

Maksud helped the Goat, still groaning, to get up, stuffed a few crumpled rubles into his hand with a careless gesture, and went back to his barrel.

"Well done, Maksud!" the bystanders clicked their tongues in approval and resumed their chatter. Like a real performer, Maksud inclined his head slightly in acknowledgment and smiled, revealing a fine row of white teeth below his narrow moustache.

The fact that Farida's shop was closed did not bother Shamanidi. It was a month since he had moved into a room of Farida's, so he had no hesitation in knocking at the back door.

"It's closed!" Farida shouted in a voice hoarse from continual swearing. "What a bloody lot of people you are!"

Shamanidi coughed. "It's me, Farida, Shamanidi." She slid back the bolt and he entered the crowded shop with its strong stench of beer. But he forgot to close the door behind him. On the other side of the window behind the bar could be seen the eager, pleading faces of the men outside. They shouted, waved their money about and begged for just a small mug to be filled, but Farida simply slammed down the metal shutter with a bang and with what seemed to Shamanidi an almost sensuous pleasure.

"When's the funeral?" Farida asked, removing her dirty apron and tidying herself up.

"The car is supposed to come at one o'clock." Shamanidi looked at his watch. "We've just got time."

"Do you want a drink?"

Shamanidi nodded. He wanted a drink all right, but he had not dared to ask the lady behind the bar.

"There's a clean mug over there," Farida said. "Pour yourself some," she added generously and even refused to take his money. Shamanidi hardly had time to blow the froth from his drink and put his mouth to the mug before the door opened and a fellow with close-cropped hair and a face covered with little white scars looked into the shop.

"Please, lovely one," he said hoarsely, "Just one little mug full—I'm dying of thirst . . . "

"Shut the door!" Farida flew at him like a racing tigress.

But at that point the man caught sight of Shamanidi in the semi-darkness of the shop and, suddenly overjoyed, cried out:

"My friend—Dimka Gevorkyan!"

Shamanidi choked on his beer.

"There are no Gevorkyans here," said Farida, pushing him out. "Don't talk such nonsense!"

"But of course it's Dimka!" the man insisted. "We were together in the same camp!"

Farida left him in peace and turned her attention to Shamanidi, who was paralyzed with fright in the corner.

"You've made a mistake," muttered Shamanidi, turning his face away. The man, gaining in confidence, pushed his way into the shop.

"Fancy you turning your back on your old friends, Dimka," he said, eyeing greedily the mug of beer in Shamanidi's hand. "That's not nice. After all, we fed on the same cabbage soup together for two years."

"What does this fellow want of me?" said Shamanidi, surprised. "The drink's affected your eyes, so go and have a good sleep."

"Even when I'm drunk I can see all right," said the man, offended. "I recognized you as soon as I saw you!"

Farida listened with ever growing interest.

"There's talk that you escaped from camp, is that right?"

Shamanidi pushed his mug of beer into the man's hand and hustled him out of the shop. "It's time for us to go," he said, trying not to catch Farida's eye. "Well, well," said Farida slowly, her eyes sparkling. "If it's time, it's time . . . "

They left the shop and Farida started to lock the door. Nearby, with his back to them, with his head thrown back like a bugler at dawn, the man who had recognized Shamanidi from their time together in the camps was greedily gulping down the beer.

From the direction of the shoemaker's hut down the street, with a strange gait, his bare feet red from the cold, came the village idiot Lyoka—a grown man who behaved like a child. Zeinab, who knew everything, would recount how he came to be like that, as the result of an unhappy love affair. The girl's parents had been opposed to the marriage of their daughter to the Jewish Lyoka. In protest, she poisoned herself, and Lyoka went out of his mind. Until then he had lived a normal life as a young engineer, and had even learned to play the violin.

Lyoka squatted down by the low window of the shoemaker's shop and for a time simply watched in silence as old Aramais got on with his work. He always enjoyed watching the old man's powerful hands handle the waxed thread and the sharp knife. Then suddenly Lyoka started to cry.

At that moment Arshik, seventeen and not very tall appeared behind Aramais's back. "What's he blubbering about?"

Old Aramais looked up from his work. "Don't tease Lyoka," he said.

"He's crying about something he's thought of," said Arshik, offended. "Tell us, Lyoka."

"I can't," Lyoka protested.

"Has someone upset you?"

Lyoka seemed to be thinking. "No," he said at last. "A lot of tears have been building up. I'm letting them flow."

Aramais beckoned him over. Fearfully and hesitantly Lyoka entered the workshop and stood expectantly in front of the shoemaker. "Give him a ruble."

Arshik delved into a tin that had previously held fruit drops but was now used for keeping small change for Aramais's customers. He handed Lyoka a few coins. "I said a ruble," Old Aramais eyed him despairingly. What a tight-fisted young man.

"I haven't got a ruble," Arshik snapped.

"You didn't give me any change back after you went to the shop."

Silently Arshik pressed a ruble into the dirty hand of the idiot boy. "Buy yourself some sweets, Lyoka."

And old Aramais gave him a friendly pat on the shoulder. "Or buy some chestnuts from old Zeinab."

Lyoka said nothing in reply. He simply clutched the money in his hand and, as usual, lifting his skinny legs high in the air, he went off down the street to a food stall near the entrance to the Armenian burial ground. "You ought to be ashamed of yourself," Aramais told Arshik without looking up.

After the death of his wife, he had adopted Arshik, then only ten years old and living in a children's home. Arshik's Armenian parents had perished in a fire. Now he lived with Aramais in his little house. Old Zeinab cooked their midday meal for them out of the kindness of her heart and also did their laundry.

The boy turned out to be a bit wild: he quit school after the seventh year and, despite Aramais's attempts to persuade him, he refused to carry on with his studies. On the other hand he took to his new father's trade with great enthusiasm. "We can't all be academics," Aramais said, giving in to the boy. "Someone's got to mend boots and shoes."

But Arshik had his own special way of exploiting his ability to make footwear. Towards evening, when old Aramais usually closed down his workshop and went to have his supper, Arshik's birdlike face with its twisted nose would peep out of the window. He would cautiously scan the whole street with his dark flashing eyes, then scramble out of the house and disappear until late in the night.

The whole district was after Arshik, and when he was caught he was beaten mercilessly. That summer alone, he had been beaten up on three occasions by a gang from the next street, and some men had set on him in the market. Nobody was at all sorry for Arshik. He deserved what he got. "He's like a mouse," said the old black-scarved women, "he steals and hides it all away."

Arshik was not a thief. Nor was he a hooligan. These distinctions were very strictly observed on the street. Real crooks like Maksud and Khobot were regarded as the upper class of the underworld, and people were afraid to get involved with them. Nor was Arshik a gangster. When he was still going to school, he never took money from children in the younger classes. He used to swap meals prepared at home for candy wrappings or, if he were paid to do it, he would eat razor blades. Arshik was a scrounger. It is difficult to give a precise definition of that word. It implied a little of everything. Scroungers walked the tightrope between what was permitted and what was forbidden by the criminal code. When he grew older Arshik began exchanging things, buying something here and selling it there, but always keeping to himself in the market or in Farida's bar. He differed from the other street scroungers by his tenacity and real fearlessness. Arshik did not squeeze money only out of the slow-witted folk from the villages: he could get it out of the thieves as well. And when at last someone caught him and pushed him into a dark corner, he was beaten close to death. But nobody ever succeeded in retrieving the money they had lost.

Meanwhile, neighbors had started to gather in the courtyard behind Aramais's workshop. The shifts in the factory had been changed for people to be able to take part in the funeral of the Beibutovs' wild son Alik, who had killed himself on his motorcycle.

The first person to appear was an Azerbaijani with the Russian name of Stepa, followed by Farida, along with Shamanidi and Rustam, his face scarred by burns received in Afghanistan. They were soon joined by Aida, an unmarried woman, wearing a fashionable jacket with wide shoulders. And, of course, old Zeinab along with the black-robed women. Beibutov himself and his wife did not turn up. The loss of their only son had put both of them in hospital with heart attacks. So it was only the neighbors who attended the funeral (for some reason, the Beibutovs' country cousins did not appear).

Old Aramais took off his leather apron over his head, revealing a powerful chest covered with gray hair, and began to change his clothes. "Are you going to the cemetery?" he asked his son, also dressed in his best clothes.

"I've got to see a man about some business," Arshik looked out of the workshop and studied the empty street attentively.

"Wait a minute, son." Aramais stopped him from leaving. "I want to talk something over with you."

Arshik frowned in irritation, thinking that his stepfather was going to ask him again about the metal tips for shoes. A man had promised Arshik that he would smuggle some out of the factory, but he had kept putting it off.

Without beating about the bush, old Aramais announced that he intended to get married. "It would be good to have a woman in the house," he said, rather embarrassed. "Without a woman a house is not a home but a barracks—you understand. Don't forget, she keeps our family going anyway—she cooks for us and goes to the market."

Arshik realized that his stepfather had old Zeinab in mind. He didn't think much of the idea. "Is it really so bad with just the two of us?" A marriage could easily scuttle the trip to Armenia they had planned to make next summer.

"With Zeinab it would be even better."

"But she's old!"

"Old for some people, not so old for others," Aramais commented quietly.

"And she's an Azerbaijani."

At that Aramais lost his temper. "There are only two nationalities in the world," he said. "There are good people and bad people. There are no others. And Zeinab is a good person. And she treats you well."

"Never mind me," Arshik said with a shrug of the shoulders. "Most important is how she treats you."

Old Aramais sighed. "That's true, son. On the other hand I think she helps us out of pity for us. For her we are like abandoned orphans."

"To hell with her then," Arshik looked down the road again.

"But if it's not out of pity?" Aramais reflected. "We were quite fond of each other even when Susana was alive. . . . You would have a woman's care and affection again. You could go to technical college . . . "

"Leave your bloody college out of it!"

"Listen, are you a complete fool?"

"I need money!"

Aramais gave him a good clout in the back of his head. "Why are you after money all the time, why?" he shouted.

"You will soon find out!"

"Let me get my hands on you!" said old Aramais threateningly. But Arshik had already slipped out of the workshop.

The old-clothes man appeared again in the street with a sack over his shoulder. Behind him came Lyoka, striding along in his usual manner. "I'll buy your old things!" the man cried out as he came to a halt in the street. Lyoka pulled out a rag doll with no arms and offered it to the man, saying in a demanding tone: "Go on, buy it!"

"Leave me alone, you silly fellow, go away," said the man through his teeth. "Get lost!"

Lyoka sniffed in resentment, put the doll away and went across to the cobbler's shop. "Here you are," he said, reaching through the open door with a sticky cheap sweet in his hand.

Old Aramais took it, and politely thanked the poor half-witted fellow.

As he went down the road, Arshik looked into the courtyard, where the coffin was already in place, on the Beibutovs' veranda. Catching sight of Shamanidi, he beckoned him over. "Have you made up your mind?" he asked when Shamanidi approached the gateway.

"I don't know, Arshik," said Shamanidi in an uncertain voice, pulling at his long nose. "I really don't know." It was true—he didn't know whether Farida would denounce him or not.

"They'll look as if they were made in Italy! With a white welt all around," Arshik said. He had made a pair of high boots and was now seeking a customer. "It's the sort of footwear for a real man to dream about. Real Caucasian!"

"I'm Greek," Shamanidi corrected him. "What about the upper part?"

"To suit the customer. We can make them very high—the 'Bottle' style—or short summer ones. Or better still the 'Polar' style with a buckle outside."

But Shamanidi still couldn't make up his mind. On the one hand he wanted a pair of warm boots, on the other he begrudged the money. He sent practically all his earnings off to his wife and child, leaving himself only enough for the bare essentials.

"And they come with a squeak!" Arshik threw in his last ace. "I have, but only for persons of substance, a well-dried and matured beech bark. We fit it in between the insole and the sole and we put brass tips on the heel and sole and, Shamanidi, you will walk, not like a Greek, but like a minister! Your boots will squeak as you walk along!"

At that moment the figures of two men could be made out at the end of the street. Arshik was immediately on his guard. "Don't worry," Shamanidi said reassuringly. "They're drinking vodka in the bar."

"Who are they?"

"A couple of your pals," Shamanidi said. "Maksud and that big fellow—what's his name?"

"Khobot?"

"That's right—Khobot."

Arshik spat. "I'm not scared of them."

"That's your business." Shamanidi again held his nose. "Anyway, in three days' time I'm going to Novosibirsk to accompany a ship full of wine from Baku—to make sure it doesn't get stolen on the way."

He had already made up his mind never to return to Sumgait. Sooner or later Farida would talk and the rumor that there was an escaped prisoner around would reach the ears of the police. There were plenty of informers among the neighbors. "Then the Polar style will be the very thing!" Arshik slapped him on the shoulder. "Everybody else will be freezing but your feet will be warm."

"How much are you asking?"

Arshik was an experienced young man. For fear of putting off the customer he never named a price at the outset. The customer had to ripen like a fig that would fall from the tree into his hands of its own accord. That was why he said evasively, "What is more, Shamanidi, since you're a neighbor, I will make you free of charge a pair of boot trees of plywood and soft cloth. You will put them in the boots every night and you'll never have a single crease in your boots or I'm a dead man."

"Your price, Arshik," the Greek insisted.

"You'll never wear them out!" Arshik continued his song.

"At the official price, then?"

"Where have you ever seen handmade winter boots, with Italian trees to them, at state prices?" Arshik said indignantly. "In Greece perhaps? I will make them look like calf!"

"Like calf?" Shamanidi's voice shook.

"Can I possibly do less for you?"

"State your price," Shamanidi said firmly and left his nose in peace. "I just want to know what your price is."

"Your goods will look as good as they cost you," said Arshik rather obscurely.

"I want to hear a figure," Shamanidi insisted.

"A hundred and fifty," Arshik half-closed his eyes. "Deposit in advance." Shamanidi gasped. "But the boots will look worth two hundred. . . . No, what am I saying, three hundred!" Arshik said quickly. "From anyone else I would ask two hundred for such individual luxury work with a white welt and metal tips."

"I can't make it," Shamanidi said sadly.

"It's up to you." They both remained silent.

"Oh, all right!" exclaimed Arshik at last. "I am not greedy, Shamanidi. A neighbor is a neighbor. A hundred and thirty, and it's a deal, right?"

Shamanidi took hold of his nose again. "It's a wonderful price. No one will make you a pair of boots for less."

"I'll have to do some thinking," Shamanidi said.

"You think," said Arshik. "Only think quickly. I've got customers lining up."

"All right, Arshik. I'll let you know on Monday." Shamanidi took his leave and went back into the courtyard.

"Oh, Shamanidi," Arshik crooned after him. "As you walk along your boots will go squeak-squeak, squeak-squeak." And, with a laugh he set off for the center of town, where Bella lived.

Arshik was pleased with himself. Shamanidi had swallowed the bait and was no doubt in his mind already walking down the frozen streets of Novosibirsk in his new boots, and the Russian women passing him and looking up in admiration at the owner of such fine footwear.

Old Aramais had changed his clothes, locked his workshop and joined the men in the courtyard. They were sitting on the veranda and smoking, waiting for the car that was supposed to carry the coffin to the cemetery. The women crowded onto the veranda and attended to the corpse. Shamanidi helped them with a grim look. Aramais sat down beside them and lit a cigarette.

As usual, the talk was of money. Deeply inhaling the smoke from a cheap cigarette, so that his cheeks sank right in, the Azerbaijani Stepa said angrily:

"Yesterday they closed down the bloody office and you couldn't get a bloody thing. But the ones who slipped him a bribe were given work. The rotten bastard!"

"And they got away with it?" inquired Rustam, a young man whose face bore the marks of having been burnt in a tank. He had recently returned from Afghanistan. "I told the brigadier: 'How can you be such a swine as to rob people you once slaved with?'"

"And what did he say?"

"He said: 'Allah isn't Yaksha—he knows who's doing badly. Push off, Stepa, and go and ask some intelligent people how to speak to your boss.'"

"People like that should be crushed!" said Rustam, his damaged face twitching.

"Where do they find such people?" Stepa growled.

"In the life we have to lead here," said old Aramais.

"Crush them!" Rustam ground his teeth. His nerves had been upset by his experiences in Afghanistan.

"I crushed him," Stepa sighed. "Word for word and some teeth got knocked out." He felt the swelling around his eye. "Like they sing in this song—'wages down and prices up.'"

"Better go and work in the oil wells," Rustam suggested, "even if it means you'll smell of oil it's more reliable than working in your building plant. Of course, you have to work over there, but you get decently paid for it."

"He's got enough strength." Old Aramais slapped Stepa on his skinny back, with a smile. "The Good Lord was kind to him."

"I was strong enough once," Stepa made a hopeless gesture with his hand. "You know very well, Aramais, that I've got two little girls depending on me." Last year Stepa's wife had walked out on him and gone off with a Georgian. "I have to keep my eyes on them, prepare their food, wash, iron and mend their clothes, and wipe their dirty noses. And on the oil wells you really have to work hard and it uses up all your energy, curse it!"

"Better get married," Rustam suggested.

"Easily said! To whom? To the sort of bitch like my former wife?!"

"Why go so far away?" old Aramais pointed to the woman Aida.

Stepa laughed. "To Aida? I've known her since we were children! We used to go swimming naked together!"

"Everything about her has changed now," said Rustam with a loud laugh. "Take a close look at her." Stepa stared skeptically at Aida.

"Why not?" Aramais supported the idea. "The girl is in her very prime. She's very straightforward and, just look, there's not a single bad-tempered line on her face."

Aida was on the veranda and sensed that they were talking about her. She glanced across at the men, blushed and dropped her head. "Go across to her and say: 'Look, Aida, it's like this . . . '" Rustam laughed again. "Come and be a mother to my children."

"Do you really see nothing at all in her, Stepa?" Aramais shook a threatening finger at Rustam.

Stepa cast another glance, this time more calculating, at the handsome girl. "She's not bad, but how can I approach her? What if she bursts out laughing?"

"I would say something like this," said Aramais thoughtfully. "'Dear Aida, we know very well what sort of people we are, since we've known each other so long . . . '"

"'Since we were both in diapers!'" Rustam interjected happily.

"'You are on your own and so am I,'" Aramais continued. "'I love you.'"

"But who said I loved her?" Stepa asked, surprised. "I quite like her and that's all."

"But does she like you?" asked Rustam.

"How can I tell?"

Old Aramais stroked his moustache thoughtfully. "Well, you can always tell by a number of signs. Her eyes smile at you when you meet in the courtyard, or she may cover her mouth with her hand when she laughs—like this, you see?" Aramais demonstrated.

"I don't recall anything about her eyes," said Stepa, wrinkling his brow. "But she certainly covers her mouth. She's got a gap in her teeth and it embarrasses her."

"But when she talks to me she doesn't cover her mouth," Rustam chipped in. "That means, Stepa, that she's fond of you. But it's got to be brought into the open." He winked at Aramais.

"But how?" asked Stepa, now getting worried.

"In the course of a relaxed conversation." Rustam stood up. "Come on—I am Aida and you approach me to carry out active reconnaissance."

"You, Aida?" Stepa said skeptically. "Don't talk daft!"

"Don't look at the scars on my face, just imagine you have Aida in place of me," Rustam insisted. "Come on!"

Stepa also stood up on the veranda, cleared his throat and in a lifeless voice said, "Aida . . . "

"Yes, Stepa?" Rustam replied in a sweet-toned voice, and gave his damaged face the most appealing expression.

Old Aramais watched his neighbors with a kindly smile. "I am listening, dear boy," Rustam encouraged the would-be bridegroom. But Stepa couldn't keep it up and burst out laughing. "Why do you have to start neighing like a donkey at dawn," said Rustam crossly. "Let's start again."

"Aida . . ."

"More tenderness!"

"Aidochka . . ." Stepa now started to take the game seriously and became rather agitated.

"That's better," Aramais said approvingly, giving Stepa the thumbs-up.

"Do you remember the meetings we used to have?" said Stepa, putting even more feeling into his words.

"They were so beautiful," said Rustam, rolling his eyes.

"In the park on the coast looking out to sea?"

"Start again!" said Rustam angrily. "Those are words out of some old song."

"But what else can I say?" Stepa snapped. "Shall I talk about how I dragged her by the hair as a child and how she complained to my mother?"

"Don't torture the lad, Rustam," Aramais intervened. "What's the point of marrying if there's no love?" He looked across at old Zeinab, who, like Aida, also felt the men's gaze on her.

"Good day to you, Aramais," she said.

The waitress Farida, the black-robed women and Aida on the veranda studied the two of them with interest. "Old Aramais's eyes misted over at once," tittered Farida and jogged Aida with her elbow.

Aramais turned away and said deliberately, "No, it's impossible without love." By marrying Zeinab he would only be making life easier for Arshik and guarding against loneliness in his old age, but he would be being unfaithful to Susana's memory.

"But you must understand," Rustam said heatedly. "She would be a mother for Stepa's children. Give the fellow a chance to breathe!"

But old Aramais did not agree. "Stepa's girls will grow up, one way or the other. They will get married and have their own families. But he will ruin his life living with someone he doesn't love. Then he'll start drinking, and it will be goodbye to his dreams of continuing his education." He turned to Stepa and asked him sternly, "Are you keeping up your studies or have you chucked them?"

"I'm studying," Stepa replied despondently. "But my work takes so much out of me that when I open a textbook at home and sit over it for half an hour, I sink into sleep as into a bog. My girls quietly take off my boots and put me to bed. I try to resist but I've no strength."

The men remained silent. "Listen, Aramais, you are urging everybody to study, your own Arshik, and Stepa, so why didn't you study yourself?" Rustam asked.

"First it was the war that got in the way. Then it was prison. And when I was released I tried to get into a technical college, but the personnel people there looked down their noses at my documents and immediately wished me goodbye."

"Yes, that's the sort of people they are," Rustam agreed. "At the entrance to our place there's a young Russian on duty, Yurka the guard. If you're five minutes late he'll snatch your pass off you."

"The bastard," Stepa interposed.

"There were guards like that in Russia even in the days of Ivan the Terrible," said Aramais.

Rustam looked around involuntarily. "You're an outspoken chap, Aramais," he said with admiration. "You've been through such terrible things in life, but it doesn't seem to have taught you anything."

"Not all Armenians are bad—there are some good ones too."

"Was it awful there?" Stepa dropped his voice. "You know—in prison?"

Old Aramais carefully tore a square out of a piece of plain paper, tipped some tobacco into it from his pocket, and skillfully rolled a cigarette. "It was awful," he said.

He had been arrested in 1947, two years after the end of the war. At the time of the anniversary celebrations, in fact. He well recalled that May Day morning. The sun was shining outside and the radio was broadcasting marches and singing the praises of the great Generalissimo. Aramais was striding around the room dressed to the nines in his dark suit, which he called jokingly his "Easter suit," a white shirt and a tie that Susana had given him for his birthday. He opened a drawer and pulled out a shoebox in which he kept his old stained documents, his medals and the Order of the Red Star. As he picked through his decorations, Aramais wrinkled his brow, unable to resolve the problem: there was no difficulty with the medals—they were held on with pins. But what about the Order? It meant making a hole in his jacket, and in a place where it would show. Of course he could fix the Order on right away and go to the parade, but what could be done with the suit afterwards? The only decent article of clothing he had would be ruined. He couldn't go around afterwards always wearing the Order. People would say he was showing off. Yet it was a pity about the suit. It was brand new and, what's more, his only one. Where would he ever find the money for another one?

Aramais fixed the decorations on to his jacket. The red Order looked very smart against the black material of the suit. He had gotten it for a real battle, the liberation of Rostov-on-Don. Aramais recalled what had happened. On the night when his reconnaissance group had been due to go out into the enemy lines there had been a snowfall. And for a scout, white undisturbed snow was worse than flares. Every movement could be detected, black on white. There were, of course, no camouflage capes: as usual they had not been brought up in time. No white capes, but a job to be done. The German unit ahead of them was being relieved, and a fresh one had arrived in its place. During the night, men on guard in the outposts had heard some suspicious movements in the enemy trenches. As it turned out later, it was a new battalion of the SS moving in. But on the night itself nobody had known that. They waited until three o'clock in the morning, the best time for a scout to operate, when the enemy would be sleeping his deepest sleep. Then they crawled out across the no-man's land. Instead of camouflage capes, they put on white underpants and vests. The approach to the enemy trenches had been studied already and a landmark had been chosen, a machine-gun post.

They made their way across a corn field that had not been cleared since the autumn, while the Germans sent up flares and released an occasional burst of machine-gun fire to show they were alert. Because of the darkness the scouts got a bit lost and, instead of arriving at the machine-gun post, they came across a rocket signaler sitting in a little trench, covered with a waterproof cape and sending his flares up into the air. He would turn back the edge of the cape, stick out his hand and, without looking, fire the flare. Aramais smiled. The German was a lazy fellow. The supporting groups with their automatics then moved up, two on the right and two on the left, and the attack group, armed with knives and revolvers, burst straight into the trench. They grabbed the German and dragged him back to their own lines. The first group withdrew and Aramais sent his own men back.

He had just turned to go back himself when a second German, whom they had not noticed in the heat of events, suddenly stood up and hurled a grenade at Aramais's men. Aramais pointed his automatic at him and shouted "Hände hoch!" The German, a very powerful fellow, struck Aramais in the side of the head and knocked him off his feet.

But even as he fell, Aramais managed to fire at the German a brief burst from his automatic. When the grenade exploded, the captured

German got away and ran back to the trench, running straight into Aramais, who had not managed to get on his feet again. The Russians ran after the German, cursing but not shooting—they wanted to catch him alive. Aramais grabbed the German by the leg and pulled him down. The rest of the Russians rushed in, tied up the German and took him off. There was a frightful noise—gunfire along the whole length of the trenches—but Aramais still managed to slip into the machine-gun post and take from his German the documents he carried.

Aramais sighed and let the hand with the Order in it drop to his side. The bad things were forgotten. All that remained from the war was what you wanted to remember. Now it even seemed to him that those had been the best years of his life. He had felt himself to be a free man then—the regime was not so demanding, there was not the constant pressure to conform, you weren't forced to lie all the time. Before moving away from the mirror on the chest of drawers he admired his reflection once again. Aramais was a fully grown man and handsome, only gray before his time.

"Susana, take a look." Aramais went into the kitchen and again held the Order against his jacket. "How do you like the look of your husband?"

"Pretty good," his wife said, gave him a fleeting glance, and went on turning the handle of the meat grinder. She had recently been out of sorts.

"That's it," Aramais said in a satisfied tone. "In those days they didn't hand out such Orders for nothing." He admired the Order again, and then said casually, "You know, I'll have to make a hole in my suit."

Susana remained silent and went on turning the handle. Her thin shoulder blades could be seen moving beneath her housecoat.

"All the other shoemakers will come to the demonstration wearing a single medal, 'For Valor at Work.' But I shall be the only one with a real wartime decoration. . . . What's the matter?" Aramais looked at his wife's bent back. "Don't you hear me?"

"Where do you want the hole?"

"About here," Aramais said busily and pointed. "Look, alongside the lapel."

"What will you do afterwards?"

"After what?"

"Afterwards—what are you going to do with the suit? Will you go around with a hole instead of the Order?"

"We can fix it easily. We'll make a little hole and afterwards we'll take it to the invisible menders. They can fix it so that no one will ever notice."

"That's what you think with that head of yours. But, you know, people aren't blind. Farida will just take one look and everyone will know."

"I would spit at Farida!"

"Spit away! You can spit at me too." And Susana went on furiously turning the grinder.

"My God," Aramais thought, pitying his wife, "what has this life done with the wonderful girl I met one day in Bulgaria?"

Every time Aramais saw Susana so tired and worn out, he felt it was his own fault. They had gotten to know each other in Bulgaria, where they had fled from the Turkish massacre of 1915, in which her father and his mother had died. They married at the end of the 1930s, and Aramais persuaded his young wife to return to the country of their ancestors. Wise old Anaid, Susana's mother, refused to go with them to Armenia. She didn't trust the Bolsheviks. "They're worse than the Turks," she said. "The Turks only kill you, but the others try to grab hold of your soul."

As it turned out, she was right. Not only Aramais and Susana, but all the emigrants from France, America and the Near East found that they were treated as second-class citizens in their native land. The authorities did not trust them, the housing situation was bad, employers were reluctant to give them work, and they were subjected to every kind of pressure. Under the Communists their motherland became a stepmother. Many of the immigrants started to go back, but Aramais and Susana were refused exit visas. So when in 1949 the authorities started sending tens of thousands of Armenians who had lived abroad to the Far North, Aramais and Susana fled from Armenia to Baku, the capital of Azerbaijan and then in their search for work found themselves in a recently developed oil town by the name of Sumgait.

"Do you realize I've got to buy a winter coat?" Susana brushed back her hair from her perspiring forehead with the back of her hand and turned to look at him with malice in her eyes. "Do you realize that, you wretched shoemaker?"

One of Aramais's eyes twitched. "Don't spoil the holiday, please. I only put a straight question to you—do they do invisible mending, or not?"

"Farida goes around in a coat with the latest artificial fur!"

"To hell with you, and with Farida too!" Aramais hurried out of the kitchen and seized a pair of scissors from the chest.

"These women have never got enough." He dug the sharp point into his jacket. "I used to earn eighty rubles, and that was too little. Now I've opened a workshop, and I bring home two hundred—and it's still too little!" Aramais shouted in the direction of the kitchen, and stuck the scissors into his jacket again. The material was new and of good quality. He made a very ragged hole in the beautiful smooth breast of the jacket and that made him even crosser. Aramais threw the scissors aside and looked at the clock. There was very little time left until the start of the parade. Muttering curses to himself, he took his medal ribbons from the box, breathed on them and polished them with his sleeve and then pinned them on to his jacket. From the kitchen he could still hear the angry noise of the meat grinder. Hastily smoothing down his hair, Aramais made for the door, where he stopped and, hesitating, shouted out: "I'm off! I'll probably be late back." And he slammed the door behind him.

Aramais came home late and dead drunk. It took him a long time to find the keyhole, and in the end it was Susana who opened the door. "Just as I thought," she said, and left it at that.

She put his heavy arm around her shoulders and helped him to his bed. There she quickly undressed him and covered him up. "Just look at your suit—my God! What on earth have you done to it?" she muttered sadly as she inspected the jacket. A cigarette had burnt a hole on the lapel.

Aramais tried to say something, rolling his bloodshot eyes around, then collapsed into the pillow. "Come to me, Susanochka. Come, mother of mine . . . " and he reached out with an uncertain hand.

"Go to sleep."

"Wait for me by the baby's bed . . . "—Aramais tried to sing a wartime song. "Kiss me, Susanoochka, come on, give me a kiss. Or are you too mean?"

Susana quickly bent over him and touched his weather-beaten face with her lips. Aramais tried again to draw close to her, but his arms fell away and he started at once to snore, his mouth wide open. "You are my big trouble," she sighed.

Having made her husband's head comfortable and laid his hands on his stomach, Susana stood looking at him for a long time. Then she wiped her eyes with her apron, covered him up with a blanket and went off to the kitchen to put a pie in the oven. They were expecting guests next day.

But that night it was quite different guests who turned up in a black Emka car with curtained windows.

It appeared that, having consumed a lot of drink at the celebration, Aramais had let it be known to one and all, in his best and most expressive army language, exactly what he thought about not only the solidarity of the workers of the world, but also about the whole of the Soviet system. And then, to underline his protest, he had flung all his decorations, including the unfortunate Order of the Red Star, into a trash can.

Seven years in labor camps and three in exile was the price that the court attached to what Aramais Yegiyants, twice-wounded sergeant of an intelligence regiment, had done.

"It was awful," Aramais repeated, lighting a cigarette, "But even there people managed to live."

"People manage to live everywhere," said Stepa philosophically. "What matters is *how* they live."

"I remember something that happened in Kabul," Rustam said. "They captured one of our parachute troops—a fellow like you, Aramais, who had been in a camp before being drafted. An Afghan woman rushed up to us, shouting and tearing her hair, complaining that one of our men was raping her daughter. Our officer took me and a couple of our tank men with guns and told her, 'Show me!' So we ran after her and she was right—the soldier had grabbed a girl and his hands were already up her skirts. The officer took him by the scruff of the neck. 'What the hell do you think you're doing, disgracing our army in the eyes of a friendly population?' To which he replied, 'I'm paying them back for killing my comrade!' We just laughed."

"Was he punished?" Aramais inquired.

"Who?" asked Rustam, surprised. "The soldier?"

"Yes."

"Oh, come on! If men were to be punished for every little trifle like that there'd be no one to do any fighting. Over there, in Afghanistan, so many stupid things were done that no one would take such a trifling affair seriously. At the outset they sent Tadjik soldiers to fight there. They thought the local population would prefer them—they speak the same language. Later they realized that the Afghans were in fact Tadjiks. It meant they were forcing brother to kill brother."

"The Azerbaijanis are also related to the Afghans," said Stepa.

"Listen, friend, when you look down the sights to aim a gun they all look the same. . . . Do you want one?" Rustam offered Stepa a cigarette with hashish. Stepa refused. "Quite right. You've got two daughters." Rustam inhaled deeply, like all hashish smokers, noisily drawing in a lot of smoke along with the air. "But in Afghanistan practically everybody started smoking the stuff. There's plenty over there."

Old Aramais studied Rustam thoughtfully. He was no longer the bright kid who had grown up in that courtyard before his very eyes. He was now a grown man with a face disfigured by war and the hard look of a man who had killed. Aramais had seen that same look in a frontline machine gunner. But in this case it looked as though Rustam's eyes had burned out because of the number of people he had dispatched to another world with his Degtyarev automatic. "Oh dear, Afghanistan!" Rustam continued to reminisce. "The things that happened to me there! It sometimes seems to me now as though I imagined it all." He looked at Aramais and Stepa with an air of childish wonder. "I've started waking up at night from the smell. I think I'm again pulling on my tankist's overalls, smelling of sweat and diesel oil. Then I feel very depressed, as though something or other . . . " Rustam sought for the right word but couldn't find it. "It was as though I had already lived the whole of my life, over there, and there was nothing more to come."

"Oh, snap out of it!" said Stepa, astonished. "Can you really ever be bored in a war?"

Rustam thought for a moment. "It's not that I got bored but that I seemed to have no purpose in life. No interest. In Afghanistan I used to have a dream: I would return home, if I managed to survive, and everybody would rush to help me. But what happened? They didn't give me an apartment, they wouldn't put me on the list for a car, and it turned out that the war had been an unjust one, whereas we had always been told at our political lectures: 'Carry out your international duty.' Well, I've carried it out, and now they all look the other way."

"They turn their heads because the war in Afghanistan is a stupid war. No one asked us to move in there."

"What's that got to do with me?" snapped Rustam. "They drafted me into the army, sat me in a tank and ordered: 'Shoot 'em and crush 'em!'"

"And what was your own head doing at the time?" asked Aramais. "You're a human being—you also have a duty to think things out."

"Oh sure," said Rustam. "The minute you start to use your head to think with, they'll screw it off you. To hell with all the bastards."

Stepa brought the conversation to an end and shouted across to the women on the veranda, "What's happened to the car?"

Old Zeinab made a helpless gesture with her hands. She and the other women had finished arranging the corpse, and were simply waiting for the car to arrive. "I must buy some tobacco before the store shuts for lunch," said Aramais, rising from his seat.

"You're right," Stepa agreed. The men moved slowly towards the gateway. Shamanidi joined them.

"Where are you off to?" old Zeinab inquired anxiously.

"To get some tobacco," Aramais reassured her, and they went off.

The women watched them go and then sat down to relax. Lyoka, lost in his twilight world, sat down beside them. The black-robed women sat silent and motionless at the coffin. "Alik was with us, and suddenly he's gone," said Aida mournfully. "The man who invented those damned motorcycles should have his head cut off!"

Farida, the waitress, blew her nose and wiped her hand on the underside of her apron. "And something else lower down should be chopped off as well!" she tittered.

"It's a sin to talk like that. But maybe Alik was lucky to have died.

Supposing he had been left a cripple, or had lost his reason like Lyoka?" Old Zeinab stroked the boy's hand tenderly. Lyoka gurgled with pleasure and he began to slobber with his lips. He loved old Zeinab. "Just think what he was like ten years ago, before he went out of his mind! He was a polite and very considerate person, and an engineer. Every evening you could see him kissing his fiancee on that corner."

"No," said Farida decisively, "I am going to put my hooligan son into a military school. They don't go riding motorbikes there. They feed them well and teach them discipline. On top of that they get a good military education."

"Quite right," said Zeinab approvingly. "Then you will have to find a husband for yourself. But who's going to take you on with a burden like your son?"

"You make good sense, Zeinab. There aren't many men nowadays who are not on the vodka, and the sober ones have become very choosy lately." Farida looked with hatred in her eyes at Aida. "These young fillies are always wiggling their bottoms—they seem to have lost all sense of shame!" She sighed. "Will you tell my fortune, Zeinab? Maybe the cards will tell me something. I dream of a long journey and an official house."

"You'd better stop putting water in the beer," said Aida spitefully, hurt by the reference to "fillies." "Then you'd stop dreaming about a house."

"So don't drink my beer then," Farida said in a strident voice, accustomed to swearing.

"I don't drink, but those who do complain about you!"

"They're not people—they are bastards. They all hang around the bar smiling but behind my back they tell all sorts of nasty stories about me." Farida turned away and pointedly addressed only Zeinab. "I was at the military recruiting office and flirted with a major there, asking him about getting my son into military school. The major always drinks beer in my bar after work, and he promised to help. I gave him a couple of bottles of very good cognac. He immediately wrote me out an application. But he said I would have to get the agreement and signature of the father."

"So let your husband sign it," said Zeinab. "He's not your son's enemy, is he?"

"He doesn't recognize him as his son."

"But you sleep together, don't you?"

"We certainly do!" said Farida bitterly. "But there's no point in it. He says he doesn't want to conceive a child when he's drunk, to make sure the child will be born healthy. But ever since he filled himself with wine on our wedding day twelve years ago he has not once returned home sober!"

"That means he loves you," said old Zeinab.

"Or hates you," interjected Aida.

"Shut up, you shameless hussy!" Farida shouted at her.

"That's what happens," Zeinab developed her thought, "A man comes home drunk, gets into bed, grunts and groans a bit, and then rolls over on his side and snores, and a handicapped child is the result. —Aida, you'd better not listen," Zeinab apologized to her young neighbor. "This sort of women's talk is not for virgin ears."

Farida gave a wheezy laugh. "Oh, Allah! She knows more about it than we do!"

Aida, offended, stood up. "I don't interfere with you, so leave me alone!"

"Stop it, both of you!" old Zeinab called them to order. "There's a dead man lying beside you and you behave as if you were in the market."

The women went silent.

"Then whose son *was* it that you brought into the world, Farida?" Zeinab herself broke the silence. She was tortured by curiosity.

"It was a delivery truck driver," said Farida reluctantly. She knew she was making a silly mistake in telling her neighbors, but the desire to share a secret was too strong for her. "He delivered a couple of barrels of beer one evening and, well, I didn't take any precautions. Only don't tell anybody. Do you hear, young lady?"

Aida chuckled. "Don't grieve about it," said Zeinab consolingly. "It means you'll have somebody to cheer you in your old age. You'll have someone to offer a glass of water to, not like the state I'm in."

"But what about old Aramais?" inquired Farida, feigning innocence. "He's still a fine, strong man, even if his hair is gray."

"You can chat, but don't let yourself be carried away," Zeinab said crossly. "Aramais can't be compared to some truck driver. He is faithful to the memory of his wife Susana."

"No need to take offense, Zeinab. I meant well in what I said. I've long forgotten what a man looks like."

"Shall I show you?" asked Zeinab with a smile.

"Go on."

Old Zeinab let her arm hang loosely between her legs. Aida was rather embarrassed, but Farida only laughed out loud. "We ought to take a photograph!" she said.

"Excuse a silly old woman, Alik," said Zeinab, bowing to the coffin.

"Wasn't it like that, Aida?" said Farida, to provoke the girl. "Or was the thing between his legs bigger?"

Aida pursed her lips. "Why do you see only that in a man?" she said coldly. "A man also has a spiritual life."

"Oh, sure," Farida agreed, "that's the pay-off!" And again she laughed in that voice of hers, hoarse and broken from the coarse language she had to use in her bar.

"Last Saturday," Aida began, "I was sitting in the public gardens reading a serious book . . . "

"She was sitting there like a worm on a fishing line, hoping to catch a man," Farida explained to Zeinab. "The book was just to make them realize that an educated woman was relaxing in a cultural way."

"Don't interfere," begged Zeinab. "Carry on, my dear."

"A man came up to me."

"What did I tell you!" said Farida triumphantly.

"He came up to me and began to speak," Aida continued, ignoring Farida. This incident in the public gardens was on her mind, and she had to have her say and hear what more experienced women thought about it. "He said very politely: 'Permit me to join you on this seat, a lonely man disturbing your peace.'"

Farida now stopped making fun of her and, like Zeinab, took in every word Aida said. "So I said to him, 'I do not associate with men I do not know,' to which he replied, 'I'm as lonely as a tree in the middle of a field.' But I said nothing, looked into my book and pursed my lips a little so he wouldn't get ideas into his head."

"But how old did he look?" Zeinab was already imagining various forms that Aida's future might take with this unknown man.

Aida made a guess. "Thirty, perhaps, maybe rather less. In a light raincoat. We make ones like it in our factory. Model seventeen."

"He's lying!" Farida announced. "He lies when he says he is a bachelor." This rather upset Aida. "Did you ever come across a case," Farida explained, "that in our day and age a man in his prime should be lonely?"

"All sorts of things can happen," Old Zeinab commented philosophically. "Maybe he had had too much to drink?"

"Of course!" Farida exclaimed, surprised that she hadn't thought of that herself.

"I don't think so," Aida said with a note of doubt in her voice. "I smelled his breath when he moved closer."

Farida cast a meaningful glance at Zeinab. "So now he was moving closer."

"You spoil everything, Farida!" Aida said indignantly.

"I'm an adult woman. I regard these things the same way men do."

"So you can tell us all about it afterwards," said Aida crossly. Then she went on, with some pride, "He suggested we should meet on the following Sunday. In the same place and at the same time in the public gardens!"

"We'll go along together," said Farida. "I'll hide in the bushes and have a look at him and then I'll tell you at once what sort of a man he is. I've got x-ray eyes—I've really been able to study these men in my bar. I can see through them all now, like panes of glass."

"I'd be ashamed."

"But Aida, you don't know anything about life! I know what men are like—just drop your guard for a moment and your skirt's over your head. You've got to be on your guard with them all the time, and most important of all, don't let their hands start mauling you all over. You only have to give in once and he'll vanish out of sight. I had one like that before I was married, when I worked in the bakery. Do you remember, Zeinab?" Zeinab indicated that she did.

"He was also very polite—he even kissed my hands. These same hands of mine." Farida held out her work-worn, weather-beaten hands, with their broken nails. "I took pity on him. I thought, 'If you only knew, my boy, how many floors I've scrubbed with these hands, how many potatoes I've dug and the mountains of dirty washing I've laundered!' Anyway, I took pity on him, took him home, cleaned him up, fed him and gave him some clothes to wear, so that he began to look like a real person, because he had been going around in just an old jacket. Yes, we lived as man and wife for a month, two months, three months, and we were already planning to get properly married. Then, one cursed day—it was a Saturday, like today—I was sitting waiting for him, looking out of the window. At last he appeared, and I called to him out of the window, 'Where have you been, you miserable drunk?!' To which he said, 'Why shout so that the whole street can hear you, Farida? It's not nice—you should be ashamed in front of the neighbors . . . ' And I replied, 'I've got nothing to be ashamed of. I've been at home all day darning your worn-out socks, while you've been away filling yourself with drink.' Then he started to lie to me: 'We were putting in an extra day at the factory for the benefit of the long-suffering fighting people of Vietnam.' But I said to him, 'Maybe you got mixed up with some woman?' At which he spat on the ground and said sadly, 'Quarreling with woman is like pissing in the wind—it all comes back at you.'

"When I heard this insulting remark, I rushed out into the court-yard, grabbed him by the arm and shouted, 'You wastrel, we're going to go before a comrades' court at your factory. Let your pre-cious collective judge us!' But when he heard that, he went as pale as a sheet and begged me pitifully, 'All right, Farida, we'll go there. Only I've just run out of smokes and I'm going to be very nervous at the comrades' court. Perhaps I could just go down to the store and buy a pack?' There was such a pitiful look in his eyes and, well, my heart is not made of stone."

"And he ran away?" Aida guessed.

"Just as he was . . . in the very same old jacket," Farida admitted gloomily. "So, Aida, you must be always on the alert. A man is like a wolf: he always wants to go back to the forest."

"He was a good man," said Zeinab sorrowfully, "polite—always the first to greet you."

"I did it for love." Farida was upset. "I wanted him to know who was boss and to be afraid to play around with other women."

"You have only yourself to blame," Zeinab disagreed. "You can be so coarse, Farida."

"That's the truth, Zeinab," Farida confessed. "Afterwards I cursed myself for it." Then, having thought a little, she added: "You could say he was the only one I really loved."

At that moment Maksud and his buddy Khobot appeared at the open gateway. They were both wearing long, unbuttoned black over-coats, with white scarves tied loosely around their necks, black patent leather shoes and huge black peaked hats. That was the way the gangs of Azerbaijanis liked to go about. "Good day to you," said Maksud, as he approached the veranda and bowed politely. Khobot hovered in the background by the gate.

The women muttered something unintelligible in reply. They didn't like Maksud, and were rather scared of him, though they had known him for a long time. In the intervals between the periods he spent in prison for armed robbery, he lived with his mother on the next street. "So we're going to bury Alik, hmm?" Maksud clicked his tongue in sympathy. "Another good boy has surrendered his soul to Allah." And with that he took off his hat and remained silent for a minute. "Has anyone seen Arshik?"

Old Zeinab made an uncertain gesture with her hands.

"And old Aramais is not around?" Maksud inquired in the same polite tone.

"He's gone to get some tobacco," said Farida. "Tell me, Maksud, why don't you come to me for beer anymore?"

"I've got trouble with my liver," Maksud complained. "I'm only allowed vodka now, and that only on holidays." He laughed, revealing a row of gleaming white teeth. "By the way, my beauties, have there been a lot of new Armenians settling in your street lately?"

"What's it to you?" asked old Zeinab, rather surprised.

Maksud put on his charming smile again. "It's like this, Zeinab. In the camp I made friends with an Armenian by the name of Vartan. A really good guy," he added warmly. "It turned out that the two of us are from the same place. His family lives somewhere in our district. He asked me to drop in on them to say hello and tell them he's safe and sound."

"Allah said you must always extend a helping hand to a good person," Zeinab agreed. "So do a good deed."

"But I've forgotten the address, you see!" Maksud slapped his forehead to mark his annoyance. "I completely forgot—I was so happy to get back to freedom!"

"Well," said Aida, "I know that the Arzumanyans were given a place in house number 25. Then the mechanic Gevorkyan got a room in the house near the Armenian cemetery."

Maksud noted this down in a little book. "There's an old Armenian woman living right next to my bar," Farida recalled. "Her son Armenak drinks beer in my place. Maybe they are relatives of your Vartan?"

"Perhaps," Maksud agreed. "I shall certainly drop in on them. Anyone else?"

"That's about all," said Aida after some thought. "You know the rest yourself."

"Oh yes, I know," Maksud agreed happily. "I wish you a good husband, Aida," he said with a wink. "A nondrinker. Better for him to have trouble with his liver. Am I not right, ladies?"

Farida let out a sigh. "Oh, sure you're right, Maksud."

Maksud put his notebook away in his pocket, went over to the coffin and again removed his hat. "Goodbye, Alik."

At that moment the men appeared in the gateway, all puffing furiously at their cigarettes. "Hello, Aramais!" said Maksud cheerfully. "How can I get hold of your Arshik?"

"Go away, Maksud," said Aramais grumpily. "I just don't want to set eyes on you."

"I've got some business to do with him," said Maksud, not taking the slightest offense. "I haven't seen him for ages."

"You have no business with Arshik."

"I owe him some money."

"What money?" Old Aramais was immediately alert.

"I borrowed fifty rubles off him," Maksud explained.

Aramais eyed him distrustfully.

"Let me be bitten by bugs!" Maksud swore. "For a pair of boots."

"Give it to me, I'll let him have it."

"Oh no—we agreed to hand it over personally."

Aramais went up to him threateningly. "Don't you try any of your funny tricks on me," he said. "And keep away from Arshik."

"Don't get worked up, old man," said Maksud, unwilling to budge. "I have weak nerves."

Aramais took Maksud by the lapel of his coat. "If you don't leave my son in peace, Maksud, you'll be sorry." With that, Khobot came striding quickly across the courtyard.

"Aramais!" cried Zeinab, rushing across to them. "Maksud, you should be ashamed of yourself, quarreling with an old man!"

The men standing around blocked Khobot's path. "You're right, Zeinab," said Maksud, apparently put out. "Forgive me, Aramais."

Aramais let him go and, with a look of disgust, wiped his hands on his jacket. Maksud took offense, his eyes blazing with anger, but he contained himself. "Once again, forgive me," and he bowed to all those present. "Say goodbye to the people, Khobot."

Khobot obediently placed his hand to his heart. Then they walked off, looking like twins in their long black overcoats and their huge fleecy hats.

Old Aramais squatted down on the veranda and lit a cigarette. His hands were shaking a little. He regretted letting himself get mixed up with the gangsters. Maksud's meekness was only on the surface. He would now get revenge through Arshik.

During his time in the prison camps, old Aramais had frequently come across just such smiling, superficially friendly but actually treacherous criminal types. Two of them, both homosexuals, very like Maksud, had persecuted a decent young man by the name of Kostya Zarubin in the Orsk camp. He had been in the next bunk to Aramais—a very trusting boy of about seventeen who had been given five year's hard labor for having typed out three copies of a novel by a Russian writer called Bulgakov, of whom Aramais had never heard. The novel bore the amusing title of *The Fatal Eggs*, and for Kostya the eggs really did turn out to be fatal. In great secrecy he gave the novel to his girlfriend to read. She showed it to her father, and Daddy, scared stiff, took the manuscript off to the secret police and wrote a report saying that a student in the first year of the university, Konstantin Zarubin, was spreading illegal literature around. Then the machine sprung into action, the wheels started to turn: arrest in the middle of the night, a search, a month under interrogation in the Lefortovo prison, and then "greetings from the far-away camps from all your comrades and friends."

This fine lad from Moscow, still little more than a boy, from a cultivated family—his father was a teacher—had taught Aramais to speak good Russian. He always laughed whenever Aramais put the stress on the wrong syllable and so changed the meaning of the word. At night time, when he and Aramais were lying side by side on their bunks, he would often recite poetry. In that dimly lit hut, crammed with suffering, groaning and snoring prisoners, it was strange to hear from his lips long-forgotten words belonging to another world—"love, tenderness, friendship, goodness." There was one poem that Kostya was especially fond of and which Aramais knew by heart:

> *Memories of what has passed*
> *Light up like flashes of summer lightning*
> *The path that we have walked.*
> *All the things that we have lived through*
> *And all the folk who have passed on*
> *Crowd like friendly ghosts into our minds.*

On one occasion, in the hut after lights-out, the two criminals began asking Kostya friendly questions about his life in Moscow, offered him cigarettes and even treated him to some bread. They reacted indignantly when Kostya told them how cruelly he had been beaten up by the security officer in his office because he had refused to become a camp informer. "All security officers are bastards," the gangsters consoled the young man.

But Aramais quickly formed the opinion that it was in fact the security officer who had sent the two of them after Kostya. "Come here," he called to Kostya.

Kostya dismissed him with a wave of the hand and went on telling the story of his meeting with the security officer and his own courageous conduct. "You're a young hero!" the thugs said in admiration. "Alexander Matrosov himself!" Then suddenly they started unbuttoning Kostya's jeans.

"What are you doing, guys?" he asked.

"What did your mother call you as a child?" one of them said, while the other continued to pull his pants off.

"Kotik . . . " said Kostya, now quite confused, as he tried to break away from them. "What are you doing?"

"Lie down, you little bastard!" The criminals flattened him out on the bunk and quickly pulled off his trousers, revealing his thin boyish legs. "Our Kotik has a lovely bum, so we'd better give him some!"

The rest of the prisoners watched what was going on and cried out, "Don't worry, Kotik—so long as you're not a queer!"

Aramais couldn't take any more of it and went over to them. "All right, you've had your fun, now stop it," he said in a conciliatory tone. The criminals were a very tough-looking pair and they probably had sharpened files or some such weapons in the pocket of their coats, so he could hardly hope to cope with them on his own. But he was sorry for Kostya. "Get out of the way, you Armenian creep!" came a shout from the depths of the hut. Aramais was blocking the view for the others who wanted to watch the free performance.

"Behave like human beings!" Aramais went closer to them, trying to decide which of the criminals to hit first. But he was beaten to it. One of the prisoners crept up behind him and struck him an awful blow across the back of the neck with a piece of wood.

As he lay on the floor, Aramais saw the rest of the scene as if through a thick fog. The gangsters gave the still-resisting Kostya a terrible beating. They ripped his clothes off his back and then, in sight of everybody in the hut, they raped him. Their passions aroused by the spectacle, some other prisoners followed suit. Aramais could not recall what followed. He crawled on his hands and knees to his place among the bunks, and lost consciousness.

He came around late in the night with a terrible headache, just able to see Kostya's pale face bending over him. "Aramais, please . . . " the boy whispered feverishly. "Aramais, what have they done to me!" Tears trickled down from his eyes, swollen from the blows he had received. "They forced me . . . " Kostya's voice trembled and he sobbed noisily. "They dragged me up on to the top bunks and tried to make me excite their organs with my eyelashes . . . And when I refused they knocked out my teeth, one by one!" He opened his mouth and revealed a gaping hole where his front teeth should have been. "Do you see?" he shouted.

"Shut up, scum," came a shout from a nearby bunk. "Let people sleep!"

Kostya hid his face in the bend of his arm and shook with silent sobbing. With difficulty, overcoming his pain, Aramais lifted himself up and passed a kindly hand over the boy's face. "Have a cry, boy," he whispered in a fatherly tone. "Just cry and then forget it all. Even this will pass, and tomorrow will be a new day."

The next morning they found Kostya hanging from a beam in the outhouse behind the hut.

But later, when the officers and men from the Vlasov army arrived in the camp, Aramais and the other political prisoners were able to turn the tables. For some time the soldiers simply studied the situation in the camp, where the criminals lorded it over all the others. Then they quickly got themselves organized, sneaked some metal bars into the camp from the mine, and one fine evening conducted a blood bath in which they beat to death thirty of the most domineering criminals. The two who had brought about Kostya's death were finished off by Aramais himself.

At last a truck stopped at the door of the house, with musicians inside. "No signs of Alik's relations?" inquired the driver, also a neighbor.

"They probably didn't receive the telegram," Zeinab suggested. "The mail doesn't work too well in the country districts."

The driver spat on the ground with feeling, to indicate his opinion of the deceased's relations and at the same time of the postal services, which were disgustingly inefficient in the towns too. "Let's have Alik, then," he said, dropping the truck's backboard.

The men lifted the coffin and carried it across the yard. The old women in their black headscarves followed. The musicians struck up a funeral march. The women began to weep, and when he saw them Lyoka started weeping too.

Nobody spoke a word at the freshly dug grave at the Moslem cemetery. They just stood around in silence. Two slightly drunk men then lowered the coffin on ropes into the grave.

The day was already coming to an end when they returned from the cemetery. The truck took the musicians away. The others stayed in the courtyard—they felt awkward about going home, and so they decided to hold a wake for Alik.

Old Aramais took off his hat, tossed some money into it and then went around to the neighbors. Zeinab told the women to go home and bring back what money they could spare. They went, but Rustam took Farida by the arm and held her back. "Wait a minute, Farida. We can't buy any drinks without you." Government regulations aimed at restricting the sale of liquor, passed a year ago, had had the effect of creating long lines of thousands of people at the shops.

Stores selling vodka at the weekends attracted the most people of all.

"What's that got to do with me?" said Farida, pretending surprise. "You can go down to the shop." Farida shrugged her shoulders, even though everyone in the district knew that she sold vodka until late at night. For double the price, of course.

"All right, Farida, don't try to kid us." Rustam handed her the money collected by Aramais. "We're all friends here—we won't tell on you."

Farida took the money, muttering, "It's always the same—they keep on begging me, but when it comes to the police it's just Farida the bar girl who gets the blame." She went into the house.

Meanwhile Aida was setting out plates and glasses on the front porch of Alik's home. Then the other women reappeared. Each one of them was carrying something for the feast—boiled potatoes, or a salad, or eggs and bread, and so on. Farida also returned. Looking cautiously around the courtyard, she pulled out three bottles of vodka from under her jacket. "Come on, folks," old Zeinab summoned them to the table.

The neighbors sat themselves down at the table. Stepa tried to place himself next to Aida. Shamanidi filled the glasses with vodka and then looked expectantly at old Aramais. As the eldest person present, it fell to him to pronounce the first parting words about the deceased.

Aramais rose, his glass in his hand. "Goodness knows how many human deaths I have witnessed—too many to count . . . " he began.

"Aida," Stepa addressed Aida in a whisper and put his hand on her shoulder. She looked inquiringly at him but didn't remove his hand. "Pass the onion, please."

"Later."

Aramais waited till they were silent and then continued. "I've witnessed it so many times, but I still can't get used to it. Each time it seems as though some vein has burst within me. Death is so very unfair. How can it happen—here was a young man, he was eating, drinking, laughing and shaking me by the hand, and suddenly he is not here! But where has he gone? What has happened to his voice, the light in his eyes, the unsaid words he ought to have spoken, the children never to be born to him? No, it is very unjust."

"And there's no one to complain to," Zeinab interposed gloomily.

"It is even worse when life is cut off quite pointlessly, as in the case of our Alik. One can understand it when it's the result of some cursed war, or old age, or serious illness, though, even then, it's difficult to grasp. For why should God have given man life, only to take it painfully away from him?" Aramais was silent for a moment, thinking over what he was to say. "But perhaps death has been given so that the people who remain alive should become better people? What I'm leading up to," Aramais tried to explain his thought, "is, although death is in itself unjust, nevertheless it cleanses the souls of other people, makes them better, kinder and more tolerant of each other. Let us remember Alik with heartfelt gratitude. He did not pass this way in vain, it might seem."

They drank the toast and started in on the food. "Would you like a juice, Lyoka?" Farida asked the idiot boy in a kindly voice.

"Yes."

"Aida, pass me the bottle, please," said Farida, with exaggerated politeness.

"Of course," Aida replied in similarly sugary tones.

Farida poured the drink for Lyoka. "Forgive me for having a sharp tongue, Aida," she said penitently.

"And you please forgive me if I cause offense." They kissed each other.

"That's the way it should have been long ago," said Zeinab approvingly.

"Our women have drunk too much," laughed Rustam. "They're kissing!"

"One minute they're barking at each other, the next they're kissing," Shamanidi said, laughing. "Women—what can you expect?"

"My dear people," said Aramais sadly, "why are you always attacking each other at the slightest provocation? Why do you never show any kindness to each other? After all, we have survived together a terrible war, destruction and hunger, so many reasons for tears—we should live together like brothers and sisters for a hundred years after all that. And did this young man have to die for us to start talking to each other like human beings and looking at each other with friendly eyes?"

The neighbors remained silent. "Sometimes you wonder," said Zeinab thoughtfully, "and you throw up your hands—what sort of fate has fallen to us? Why does every little trifle seem like a gift?"

"But I imagine what our life will be like in the future." Aida looked at Stepa, who already had his arm tightly around her in a possessive manner. "Every day, even on Mondays, people will be walking down the street, all of them smiling. Well-dressed and beautiful to look at, like a holiday. They'll actually receive butter on their ration cards. The shops will be full of all kinds of sausages, various cheeses, and meat—have as much as you like!" She became rather flushed from the very thought of what a wonderful life it would be.

"And everyone will have their own separate homes," said Farida shyly. It was so unexpected to hear something like that from such a loud-mouthed woman that the neighbors exchanged glances. "With a bathroom and a toilet just for two families."

"With a toilet!" said Rustam mockingly. "You're having some fancy ideas, Farida!"

"I'm already in my thirties, my dear Rustam, and I would just like to live in decent conditions."

"Most important is the worldwide brotherhood of the working people!" said Rustam with feeling, repeating what had been drummed into his head from childhood. "Plus the absence of the unemployment they have in the capitalist countries!"

"Keep that for your political meetings," Stepa admonished him. "Folks here don't need their brains washed. I'll be damned if—" Then he remembered he was sitting next to his future wife and he stopped short. "What I mean is, to hell with the capitalist world. It would be good if we could work on the same shift!" And he kissed Aida.

The company burst out laughing and the black-robed women with one accord lifted their parchment-like faces from the table and started whispering. "Just remember you're at a wake, Stepa," Zeinab admonished him.

"Life and death—they always go hand in hand," commented old Aramais. "I don't think Alik would have taken offense."

It was the afternoon of February 27, 1988. The people sitting around the table were united by a feeling of age-old human sympathy, and it was reflected in their faces.

FIVE

On February 26, the day before the events in Sumgait, three men, all Azerbaijanis, met in one of the higher-class buildings on the waterfront in Baku. They arrived one at a time, taking great precautions and using only public transport. But from their appearances, you could be sure that they all had the use of official cars with their own personal drivers.

At short intervals each of them went up in the elevator and opened the door of the apartment with his own key. The three-roomed apartment was equipped with good furniture, and included a large kitchen that sparkled with cleanliness. A double-refrigerator of German make was stuffed with every kind of delicacy, including red and black caviar, and the bar in the sitting room contained innumerable bottles of liquor, all with foreign labels. But despite all these signs of plenty and good housekeeping, there was a feeling about the place, difficult to define, that it was not lived in but was used for other purposes.

The three men exchanged handshakes and sat down at a table. "The situation is always getting more complicated, so we must go into action today," the first man said, without any preliminaries. He was the man from Baku who had flown to Moscow in January. "It would be good to start immediately after the lunch break in the plants that work on Saturdays."

"Wouldn't it be better to do it before lunch?" the second one objected. He was a man with a rather delicate style and ingratiating manners. Unlike his two colleagues, who were dressed in formal suits and in collars and ties, he was wearing a fashionable jacket and a silk shirt. It made him look like either an artist or a poet. "People are worse-tempered when their stomachs are empty."

The third man nodded in agreement. There was no mistaking the fact that he was a military man. Even in a well-upholstered armchair he managed to sit upright in his tightly fitting gray jacket. What's more, his gestures were short and abrupt. "I agree with you."

All three of them avoided using each other's names. "Well then, the day is decided on and so is the time, roughly," said the man from Baku. "So now I suggest we go briefly through the main points in the forthcoming events."

"But we've been through them many times already."

"As our dear Russian brothers like to say: 'Measure seven times— cut only once,'" the man from Baku said with a grin.

"It's a very serious business," grumbled the military man.

"Then let's start with you," the man from Baku turned to the man with the ingratiating manners. The latter took his glasses and a note-book from his pocket. The soldier eyed the notebook with disapproval but said nothing.

"First of all, in order to prepare public opinion in a suitable way, we have written and published in the press numerous articles and scholarly monographs by historians proving convincingly the right of Azerbaijanis to the territory called Nagorno-Karabakh. Secondly—" the one who looked like an artist coughed—"to provoke Armenians to butcher the hundred and sixty thousand Azerbaijanis living in Armenia. This will be easy to achieve, bearing in mind the forthcoming events in Sumgait."

The soldier could bear it no longer. "You're a grown man!" he said. "Imagine putting such things down on paper!"

"What's that?" said the man who looked like an artist, but who was in fact a quite well-known journalist in the republic. The soldier scared him. "Oh, yes, of course—right away . . . " and he took a cigarette lighter out of his pocket.

The man from Baku stopped him. "You'll have plenty of time. Read us the notes you've got there. What made you decide to pick that particular town?"

"Sumgait is one of the most unattractive towns in our republic," the journalist, now calmer, explained. "A lot of dispossessed elements, former criminals from prison camps, have been attracted by the oil refineries. The town is badly supplied with food. Housing conditions are appalling."

The man from Baku frowned. Like every Party leader, he didn't like to hear people talking about the population's social problems.

"True, the ecological conditions are very bad—the air in the town is extremely polluted. At the same time, however, there are enough successful, wealthy Armenians—doctors, lawyers, businessmen. . . . In short, it will be sufficient to strike a match in Sumgait for there to be a real conflagration. We'll roast the Armenians on that fire. The wind will be blowing in the right direction." The journalist took a breath and cast his eyes on the bottles in the bar. He had a constant desire to assuage his feelings with drink to get rid of the fear that tortured him. This feeling had been with him since the day he had agreed to take part in this frightful game. But his two interlocutors were eyeing him expectantly, and the journalist didn't have the courage to go to the bar. "In this way the masses will work off their feelings, not on the Soviet regime or the Communist Party of Azerbaijan"—he nodded slightly in the direction of the man from Baku—"but on the Armenians. They will be egged on by the long-standing religious animosity of the Moslem Azerbaijanis to the Armenians, who preach Christianity."

"That's all empty theoretical chatter," the military man interjected. "What practical steps have you taken?"

"There's no such thing as practice without theory," the journalist commented pointedly, but did not pursue the argument. He knew how awesome a military organization the man represented. "As for practical measures, so-called 'shock groups,' each of five to seven men, have been formed in every district of Sumgait. Their job is to rally indignant crowds of Azerbaijanis and direct their actions."

"How are they going to find the Armenians in such a big town—are they going to ask people to see their passports?" the military man inquired. "Or will they go by the size of their noses, which are no smaller in the case of the Azerbaijanis than the Armenians?"

"The aroused instinct of a true Moslem will tell them!"

The soldier grinned. "You can leave that demagogy for your next article. Tell us in concrete terms!" The journalist shriveled up inside. He really had got himself into deep trouble. It was too serious a gamble he had got himself into, and if he were to try and get out of it now he could expect no mercy from such a man. Oh, Allah! How tranquilly life had flowed before! A high salary, a beautiful apartment, a cottage practically on the sea front, and another very cozy little room that he rented especially for his mistress. Paid trips to Moscow and Leningrad, where he always stayed at the best hotels and had a wonderful carefree time going out to restaurants with a couple of good-looking models. What the hell had prompted him to get mixed up in big-time politics?

"Well?" the soldier pressed him.

"This is the fifth day that specially chosen people have been drawing up lists, going around from house to house and meeting the genuine patriots. We learn from them where and in which flats the Armenians live. We have also taken account of the time of day. If events begin to take off in the evening, the Azerbaijanis who have been warned in advance will switch off the lights in their houses. The lights that stay on will indicate to our activists exactly where the faithless Armenians live. A safe spot has been selected for the operational staff. There, incidentally, we have stored dozens of posters and banners calling on the Azerbaijanis not to be led astray by the tricks of the Armenians, and to fight for Nagorno-Karabakh. We shall give them out tomorrow morning. That's all from me." The journalist tore the pages out of his notebook, lit his lighter and burnt his notes for all to see.

"It's better like that," said the soldier, as he watched the procedure and stirred up the ashes in the ashtray with his fingers.

"Now we'll hear what you have to say," the man from Baku said.

"The police, employees of the local KGB and the army units stationed in Sumgait will adopt a neutral position."

"That's most important," the man from Baku stressed.

"I understand," the soldier agreed. "But, so that it will not be possible later to accuse us of obvious inactivity, a few Armenian families in different districts will be given protection. That will not alter the general situation, but it will provide us with excellent cover."

The man from Baku nodded approvingly.

"Further, it is not entirely impossible that the Armenians will quickly realize what is happening and will succeed in joining together and putting up some resistance. People in desperation will fight to the death. If they come up against that kind of opposition the crowds on the streets may retreat. None of them will want to risk his life. This has also been taken care of. Through your operational center in Sumgait," the soldier nodded in the direction of the journalist, "the senior shock groups will be issued with firearms. That will give them self-confidence. Especially since the numbers on the guns are not recorded anywhere."

"How on earth did you manage to get hold of them?" The man from Baku was curious.

The soldier grinned. "We have to thank our smart Geider Aliyev for that. He knew that the time would come when the Azerbaijanis would need weapons."

"Well now . . . " the man from Baku massaged his temples with his fingers. "We will not, I presume, go into greater detail."

"There is one other important question that bothers me," the soldier said firmly. "It concerns you. Can't you explain to us what Moscow's attitude is? The people in Moscow are quite capable of dropping parachute units on Sumagait five hours after the outbreak of disorder. It would take them a matter of minutes to disperse the crowd."

The man from Baku did not want to talk about his relations with Moscow, especially about his meeting with Number Two. But it was a reasonable question and it demanded an answer. "I can tell you only one thing," he said. "Not a single military transport aircraft with 'blue berets' in it will take to the air in the course of three whole days."

"But how will the local Party authorities in Sumgait and the Central Committee of the Party in Baku react?" the journalist inquired.

"That's my worry," the Baku man said through his teeth. "Don't worry your head about it."

"I'm sorry," muttered the journalist, realizing that he had put his foot in it.

"Watch the program 'Vremya' on your television and you'll understand," said the Baku man, in a more friendly tone. The journalist's obvious alarm had canceled out the lack of tact in the question.

"Well," he said, looking at his watch, "It's time to go."

They all rose. "Although I have long been a Communist and an atheist," the man from Baku smiled, "I shall say nevertheless: 'May Allah help us.'"

"Amen," said the others.

After leaving the meeting the journalist returned home, lunched with his family, seized the little suitcase his wife had already packed for him, kissed his children goodbye and went out onto the street.

A brand new car, the latest and most expensive model of Zhiguli, stood in front of the house.

The last thing the journalist wanted to do at that moment was to drive to Sumgait and there, after his few minutes of domestic tranquillity, get involved in those dangerous affairs. "But in the end," he reflected philosophically, as he got into the driving seat, "life has to serve us, we don't have to serve life." So he decided first of all to pay a visit on his mistress and then carry on to that cursed town. He turned the ignition and drove off.

The journalist was not experienced in the ways of the secret police and consequently did not notice that he was being followed by two other cars that took turns tailing him. Even if he did notice it, he attached no importance to the matter. He was far too confident in the power of the people with whom he had been meeting that morning.

He and Nina, his mistress, usually liked to perform in bed as follows: they would turn on a video player and watch a pornographic film. Once aroused by what was happening on the screen, they would put the film on hold and copy the pose that had pleased them. Unfortunately, without this psychological stimulation the journalist didn't feel able to perform like a real man, despite how attractive Nina was. The journalist had met her at the television station, where she worked as an assistant to a producer.

As soon as he arrived, they started to limber up. Her heels clattering on the parquet floor, Nina went up to a big mirror, raised her hands above her head and let down her chestnut hair. Her light housecoat slipped from her shoulders to reveal her magnificent, tanned body. Her long legs were encased in tights, with an opening that revealed a dark triangle of pubic hair. The journalist also removed his clothes and embraced Nina.

At that very moment, there was the sound of a camera shutter clicking several times in succession, and a voice said quietly, "Bravo."

Nina cried out in fright. The journalist pulled quickly away from her and looked around.

In the doorway stood a strange man in a dark gray raincoat and hat. "Bravo," Major Simonov repeated, clapping his hands, having put his camera away in his pocket. "Scenes like that have an effect on me, even in the course of carrying out my official duties."

"Who are you?" asked the journalist, jumping to his feet and holding up his falling trousers.

"I'll tell you in good time." Simonov gave a signal.

His colleague from the hallway took hold roughly of Nina, who was dazed by what was happening, and led her into the kitchen.

Simonov closed the door firmly behind them and sat down in the armchair opposite the journalist, who was feverishly putting his clothes on. "I suggest," the major said, "that in ten minutes we will leave and you can carry on with your very original games. Yes, do sit down, there's no virtue in standing up. Virtue is in this thing" –and he took the camera out of his pocket again.

"Do you know who I am?" the journalist asked, having at last gotten control of himself. "I'll see you rot in jail!"

The major took a developed photograph out of the Japanese camera and showed it at a distance to the journalist. "Would you like to have a look?" the major offered. "Or would you prefer to study it along with your wife, who would certainly be glad to have this photograph as a souvenir?"

The journalist said nothing. The picture showed him and Nina together down to the smallest detail. "When someone remains silent for a long time," the major commented with satisfaction, "it means that he is very soon going to talk a great deal. You can trust my experience."

Simonov turned out to be right. Half an hour later, the journalist had not only recounted what had taken place at the meeting that morning and informed the major in detail of the events due to take place in Sumgait, but he also had signed an agreement to collaborate with the KGB.

It was already high noon when Sevda pointed out a signpost that read "Kazakh-Idzhevan."

"This is the frontier between Armenia and Azerbaijan."

If Levon hadn't said this, Gerald would not have paid any attention to that very unimpressive place. The road wound its way through the mountains beneath overhanging cliffs burnt dry by the sun. They had driven through one pass after another, each one steeper than the last. Occasionally they could see in the valleys impoverished-looking villages with houses made of gray blocks. The Armenian villages did not distinguish themselves in any way from the Azerbaijani ones. There were hardly any men to be seen in either of them. Only elderly women could be seen sitting in the doorways, with their deeply creased faces burnt almost black from the sun. They were cleaning corn cobs, following the dust-covered car with their eyes until it was out of sight. Sometimes the outline of a humble little Armenian church clinging to the cliff would suddenly come into view.

It all left Gerald with a feeling of time having stood still, and of the futility of existence. "Russia has suppressed these people with an iron weight," Gerald thought. "The Armenians have outlived all the others—the Sumerians, the Romans and the Mongol hordes, but in only seventy years of the Soviet regime the Communists have succeeded in driving one of the most ancient people of the world into a corner. Armenia needs to find a sure way out of this situation. Otherwise, like some primitive people, they will simply pass, quietly and unnoticed, out of history altogether. It is young people like Levon and Sevda, strong and uncompromising, who must take her fate into their own hands."

On the way they admitted to Gerald that they were members of the semi-legal youth organization known as "SAS," the Union of Armenian Students. The Union considered that its main task was the restoration of Armenia's sovereignty as an independent state. "God grant that they should succeed," said Gerald to himself, as he studied the girl's long white neck and the attractive curl of her hair.

Sevda drove the car with confidence. "I wouldn't mind taking her with me back to America." The thought came unexpectedly into Gerald's head. "It's time, as military people like to say, to start digging a second line of trenches. So that there should be someplace to return to after trips abroad. They say that Armenian women make faithful wives. Perhaps fate is giving me a sign by arranging this trip and the meeting with Sevda? After all, I'm over forty now, and it's time to look for a harbor in which to drop anchor."

Its engine overheating from climbing so many hills in low gear, the car surmounted the last pass and started to drop down, using the engine for a brake.

Gerald stretched and yawned. "We'll soon be there," Levon said, turning him from the front seat. "Not much further."

Sevda suddenly stopped the car on the edge of a precipice. "Look!" she exclaimed anxiously.

Down below could be seen a green valley with patches of cultivated land. There were two villages, one on each side of the valley, each clinging to the hillside and separated by a narrow but fast-running stream. A side road led to the villages from the main highway. From where they stood Gerald could see two huge crowds of people armed with big sticks and pitch forks running towards each other across the bridge. A minute later they had collided with each other and started a merciless battle. "That's Azerbaijanis fighting Armenians," Levon said. "Let's go there!" And he clenched his fists.

Sevda refused. "Our business is more important than a fight," she said. "We don't have the right to get Gerald mixed up in that sort of affair."

But Gerald had already jumped out of the car, aimed the camera at the crowd and begun clicking away.

The shouts of the embattled people did not reach to where they had stopped, but the telephoto lens brought their enraged, blood-stained faces and their wide open but silent mouths very close. They could see the sticks, pitchforks, spades and fists. As he recorded on film the massive slaughter that was going on, Gerald could almost feel physically the breaking of bones down below and the people maddened and choking with hatred. But the dust raised by hundreds of feet gradually concealed the fighting and the awful scene faded away.

Shaken by what they had seen, they continued on their way in silence. For a long time Gerald could still see with his mind's eye the furious faces of the people killing each other. He understood for the first time what was meant by crowd hysteria. It was a frightful thing.

But Gerald could still not understand what it was that sustained so strongly the hatred in those embittered people. Was it because they belonged to different nationalities? Gerald had English, German and even Jewish blood flowing through his veins, but neither he nor his friends ever attached any special significance to this. His parents were equally indifferent to the question of nationality. "It's of no importance what you are by nationality. So long as you are a decent person," his father, a wise man who had seen a great deal in the course of his life, used to say.

"What does membership of a particular nationality mean, after all, in our twentieth century?" Gerald asked himself as he looked out of the car window. "Technical advances—newspapers, radio, television—have swept away what used to be strictly defined frontiers between peoples. They have developed in people of all nationalities a common way of thinking and of looking at the surrounding world, and have even dressed them in identical clothes. An excellent example of this is provided by the people of Europe and, of course, the United States, whose population consists almost entirely of émigrés from other continents. It is scarcely possible nowadays to distinguish the outlook of a Frenchman from that of a Swiss, an Englishman or a German. In practice it can be done only by reference to the fact that they speak different languages and enjoy a different cuisine. The German prefers to drink beer and eat sauerkraut and pig's trotters, while the Englishman prefers eggs and bacon and also drinks beer. Only the culture remains national. And as they develop economically and socially the countries of the Third World tend also to adopt European standards. It is economic backwardness and to a certain extent religious prejudice that is preventing other peoples from achieving a European level. But it is just a matter of time. Cosmopolitanism—that is the future of the whole of mankind. In general, a person's country is where he feels free. Unless, of course, a new war destroys the whole of civilization."

Stepanokert, the capital of the Nagorno-Karabakh region, greeted them with deserted streets and armed patrols. There were tanks stationed at the main intersections, which Sevda sensibly avoided, and the barrels of their guns were aimed menacingly down the length of the main highway. All the town's main offices, factories and schools were closed down—the people were on strike. There were only a few food shops open, and their shelves were practically bare. They had nothing apart from bread and some cereals.

Levon asked Sevda to stop the car at a phone booth. He called someone and, back in the car, gave Sevda an address. They wound their way around the back streets until they found the street they needed. The man they were seeking was a rather fat, elderly Armenian with a graying crewcut and the badge of a deputy to the regional soviet in the buttonhole of his jacket. He met them at the gate of his little private house. After a suspicious glance at Gerald, he beckoned them inside.

He was a sullen and not very communicative character, but he described briefly and very clearly the situation that had developed in Nagorno-Karabakh. Gerald gathered from this that the aim of the local Party and government authorities, who received their orders from Baku, was to drive the indigenous population—that is to say, the Armenians—out of the region altogether. They would then settle this fertile region entirely with Azerbaijanis.

To achieve this, every possible kind of discrimination was being employed. In the schools and other educational institutions the study of the Armenian language had been removed from the syllabus. The building of a television station intended for the reception of programs from Armenia had been halted. Theatrical companies from Yerevan were not allowed to perform in Stepanokert or the other towns in Nagorno-Karabakh. Various excuses were found for not appointing people of Armenian nationality to important posts. The man cited many more examples, with Sevda translating quietly into English.

"You have to understand the difficult and humiliating conditions in which we live," the plump Armenian said to Gerald. "You must realize that seventy-five percent of the population of Nagorno-Karabakh consists of Armenians. Because of that there are continual conflicts. Today the whole town is on strike."

"You can't fight for national rights and at the same time be clubbing a person of a different nationality down," Gerald said, and he went on to describe the battle between two Azerbaijani and Armenian villages that they had witnessed on the way.

The Armenian frowned. "I don't know who started the fighting you saw," he said. "But it was the defense of our national rights that we thought of first of all. We deputies called together a session of the regional soviet, in strict accordance with the law, and passed a resolution to the effect that Nagorno-Karabakh should be joined to Armenia. The situation seemed to be favorable for this. As you know, Gerald, the process of a democratic reconstruction, or *Perestroika*, is now taking place in the country."

Levon and Sevda exchanged glances and made skeptical noises. "Oh yes, I know," the man said angrily, having noticed their reaction. "I shouldn't bring *Perestroika* into it, I know, but after all it exists. Could such a session of the soviet conceivably have been held a couple of years ago? The whole lot of us, along with our immunity as deputies, would have been rotting in jail!"

"It can still happen," muttered Levon, and Gerald understood what he was hinting at.

"Does it not seem to you that the events in Nagorno-Karabakh have become a factor in the destabilization of the policy of *Perestroika* announced by the government?"

"I would have phrased the question differently," the older Armenian argued. "Nagorno-Karabakh has become a touchstone for *Perestroika*. That is where democratic principles are being tested for their strength."

"Do you consider that *Perestroika* has withstood the test?"

The Armenian hesitated. "For the time being," he said reluctantly, "because of the old Stalinist inertia, it doesn't really work."

"In the Soviet Union today I find that everything negative is happily put down to Stalin's rule," Gerald pressed the point, sensing a weak spot in the Armenian's position. "Supposing it is not inertia, but the true face of the present government that the media are not painting with attractive slogans about *Glasnost* and democratization?"

The Armenian was a man who had lived through a great deal and, was by virtue of his age, very careful. So he gave an evasive answer. But Levon voiced his opinion with directness and feeling. "They're afraid of creating a legal precedent. If they returned Nagorno-Karabakh to Armenia, Moscow would have to give back to the deported Tatars the land that belongs to them in the Crimea, and, most important, permit the Baltic republics to regain their independence.

To let Lithuania, Latvia, and Estonia become the independent states they were before they were occupied by Soviet troops!"

"There is yet another consideration," Sevda remarked. "Moscow doesn't want to upset the fifty million Moslems inhabiting the territory of the Soviet Union."

"What do you mean by 'upset'? There are laws in the constitution to deal with that—" Gerald was about to continue, but Levon cut him off with a laugh:

"Have you really still not understood anything about our life here?"

"OK, I give in," said Gerald. "Then just answer one final question," he was addressing the Armenian. "You are a deputy to the regional soviet, that is to say, a person officially elected by the people. What is your attitude to the work of the illegal 'Karabakh' committee, which also speaks on behalf of the Armenian people?" Not only Gerald but Sevda and Levon too were curious to hear his reply.

The Armenian remained silent, stroking the smooth back of his neck with his hand.

"The Soviet authorities accuse them of playing politics and of exploiting for dishonest ends the passions that have flared up around the future of Nagorno-Karabakh. Do you take the same view?" asked Gerald.

"I'll tell you one thing," the Armenian said in a firm voice. "God grant that all Armenians were such worthy people as the members of that committee. They have earned the deep gratitude of all the people of Karabakh. Put that in your newspaper. And finally I would just like to emphasize that I believe that sooner or later the question of reunification of Nagorno-Karabakh with Armenia will be decided in a positive way. The constitutional, historical and simply moral right is on our side. The Politburo and the government of our country understands this."

"Like a true Soviet person," said Gerald with a scarcely detectable smile, "you have faith in the future."

"Yes, I'm a member of the Party," the Armenian agreed, but without catching the tone of Gerald's statement.

"Then, as a member of the Party," Levon said with venom in his voice, "explain to me why Moscow has brought the conflict between the Azerbaijanis and the Armenians to the present critical state."

Gerald looked at Levon with approval. The same question had occurred to him.

"Our two peoples have been put on bad terms with each other for ages," Sevda added her word, "but why should the situation end in bloodshed? A fight between two villages can be the beginning of a big tragedy!"

The big Armenian muttered something unintelligible about reasons of state that ordinary people could not know about, that took the interests of the Azerbaijanis into consideration, about foreign policy aims, and so forth.

"The overriding interests of the state and the policy of the government," Levon commented, stressing every word, "are above all to observe our own laws and to promote the happiness and well-being of the people, both Armenian and Azerbaijani, not to encourage bloody murder between them!"

The quarrel was becoming more heated, and threatening to develop into personal hostility, but it was interrupted by the appearance of the Armenian's wife in the doorway. She invited them to eat lunch with them. Having caught sight of the bottles of brandy set out on the table, Gerald turned down the invitation, almost in fright. He had not forgotten the frightful drinking bouts in Yerevan. Levon and Sevda also thanked the couple but did not accept. Reacting to the puzzled looks on the faces of the Armenians, Gerald explained that he had still to meet a lot of people in Stepanokert, and return to Yerevan as quickly as possible. Otherwise the KGB would alert the whole of its organization, and that could threaten not only him but also Sevda and Levon with serious trouble. "If you don't object," said Gerald, "we will just take a snack for the road."

The woman was offended, but she wrapped them up a couple of chickens, some Armenian green salad and, of course, a bottle of three-star brandy.

The Armenian accompanied them to the gate. "I hope you will find it possible to report objectively on our misfortunes, our sorrow and our humiliation," he said.

"I am not Soviet television," said Gerald jokingly, shaking the hand extended to him.

When the car had moved away from the house, Levon said in a tone of disappointment, "There you are now—he is a decent, honest fellow. But he's an orthodox Communist. People like him served prison sentences under Stalin, but they still shout 'Long live the Soviet regime!' And they defend any stupidity performed in the country by Communists!"

"There are people like that, who cannot live without a faith," Gerald tried to come to the defense of the Armenian deputy. "This fellow is really unfortunate. His whole life is torn apart by contradictions. Some people need a god, others bow before an ideology."

"Let them believe in the good and the well-being of their own people," said Sevda. "And let them fight for that."

"They fight, but they do it in accordance with the demands of their philosophy," Gerald argued, and then said thoughtfully, "To understand is to forgive. That man is of a different generation from yours."

There was something else on Gerald's mind, too. "I didn't want to say this in front of our host, but I will say it to you. All right, Armenia has cut itself off from the Soviet Union and has become independent. Then who is going to help the Armenians recover the territory seized by Turkey and Azerbaijan? America? The United Nations? World public opinion?"

"We will do it ourselves," said Levon.

"I don't want to offend your national feelings, but Armenia is hardly strong enough to oppose the whole hostile Moslem encirclement. Turkey on one side, Iran on the other, and an embittered Azerbaijan next to you. Without Russia you will be left alone in a sea of Moslem hatred."

"So it follows that our people are condemned to be forever a part of the Soviet Union?" Sevda inquired bitterly.

"The Communist regime in Russia will not last forever. It seems to me that it is precisely the Armenians who have made a deep crack in that reinforced concrete system. You were the first of all the republics to oppose the total oppression of peoples by the Soviet regime. But, I repeat, the situation is very complicated—and dangerous."

"And there is only one way out of it," Levon said firmly. "And that is for our people to be united. To become a single unit. And we are capable of doing it. The latest events in Armenia and Nagorno-Karabakh have shown that the Soviet regime has not killed off the freedom-loving spirit of the Armenians."

"There will be a lot of bloodshed. Don't you fear the responsibility?"

"You cannot allow a people to be buried alive and to beat their head against a coffin lid for so many decades. Our children would never forgive us for that. We've got to start somewhere."

They had not gone far when they were stopped at a roadblock by an officer of the traffic police and two soldiers in bulletproof jackets with automatics slung over their shoulders. The officer stepped off the pavement and signaled them to stop with a casual wave of his baton. He walked around the car, felt the lid of the trunk, and only then indicated to Sevda that she should produce her driver's license. The soldiers stayed some distance away and lit cigarettes.

"The officer is an Azerbaijani," Levon whispered. Gerald was always surprised at the way Armenians, Georgians or Azerbaijanis could tell at a glance each other's nationality.

Sevda dropped the window and handed the officer her license. "And what is a car with Yerevan registration doing in our town?" inquired the officer after he had studied her document.

"I have got relatives living in Stepanokert," Sevda replied.

"It's good to have relatives," the officer commented in a serious tone. "On which street do they live?"

"Am I being interrogated?"

"What are you taking offense about, young lady?" the officer asked, mock good-naturedly. "I know everybody here and I would have told you how best to get to your relatives." Despite his round face and apparent good temper, he was not as simple as he looked. "By the very shortest route."

"I know my way."

"It's very good to know that such a young and pretty girl knows everything," the officer said, with a not entirely intelligible note in his voice. "And who are these people?"

"My friends."

"It's good to have friends," said the officer as he continued to inspect Levon and especially Gerald, in whose appearance he had immediately detected something unusual for a Soviet person. Most likely it was the indifferent expression on his face in the presence of a man in the uniform of a policeman. "Do you have your documents, friends?"

"You are only a traffic cop. You have the right to ask for the documents only of the driver!" said Levon indignantly.

"There's a bad situation in town at the moment," the officer explained calmly. "All sorts of nasty people come down here and start exciting the population." And he repeated more insistently, "Your documents, please."

Levon shrugged his shoulders and showed his student card. "Clever boy, studying in the university," the officer said approvingly. "And you, my friend, where are you studying?"

Gerald looked at Levon, at a loss what to say. But Sevda quickly jumped in. "He's deaf and dumb," she said, "from childhood."

In confirmation of what she'd said, Gerald made strange noises in an apparent effort to speak and gesticulated with his hands. If the officer had heard his foreign accent he would have taken him at once for a spy.

"Oh dear, poor fellow," said the officer sympathetically. "He wears such an expensive suit and has such an expensive toy, and yet can't speak." And he reached for the Nikon camera. "Let me have a look—I've never seen one before."

But Gerald hid the camera behind his back. "He's deaf and dumb, but he doesn't trust me," the officer said, deeply disappointed. "Oh well, if he doesn't want to show me he doesn't have to." Then he added in a reasonable tone, "Deaf and dumb people also have to carry documents. So where are they?"

"Listen," said Sevda "I haven't committed any traffic offense. What else do you want of us?"

"Give him some money," said Levon in Armenian. "He's only trying to get a bribe out of us."

The officer glanced across at the Russian soldiers and said, also in Armenian, "An Azerbaijani officer does not take bribes from Armenians."

"If he doesn't, then he's not an Azerbaijani," commented Levon.

The officer's eyes narrowed. "That's not nice—you're insulting me. And I have my orders—to stop all cars with Armenian numbers and accompany them to headquarters."

Sevda suddenly stretched out her hand through the open window, snatched all the documents from the astonished officer, and shot off at top speed.

Behind them they could hear the police alarm whistle followed by a warning burst of automatic gunfire. But Sevda had already swung around a corner and made the car go even faster. Now there could be no more talk of meeting people in the town. They would have been arrested. The officer would certainly have made radio contact with all the traffic control posts in the town and given descriptions of the people in the car. They also would naturally have closed the main road to Yerevan.

Until it was dark they hid the car in a little forest on the outskirts of the town. Sevda and Levon spread out a map and tried to work out the best way to get out of Stepanokert, and came to the conclusion that the safest route, although it was sixty miles longer, was along the old abandoned road to Georgia, through Azerbaijani villages. If the villagers caught sight of a car with Yerevan registration they might well attack it. But there was no other choice, and once it was dark they set off.

"Look, friends," said Gerald, convinced that they were now clear of the town. Producing his exposed films, he continued: "These films are documentary proof about the events in Nagorno-Karabakh. I'm afraid that in Yerevan the KGB might confiscate them by force."

"Give them to me," Levon suggested immediately. "I'll hide them."

Gerald thanked him. It was exactly what he had intended. "We'll do like this," said Gerald after handing Levon the cassettes. "I will get out of the car at some railway station before we get to Yerevan and I'll make my way there by train. Nobody must see us together."

"So long as they haven't been informed by Stepanokert," Sevda switched on the headlights. They had already been driving for an hour and had not met a single car on the road.

"Hardly," Gerald disagreed with her. "I reckon that Azerbaijani officer stopped us by chance. He simply noticed the unusual number."

Levon nodded. "Send me the films to Moscow with a reliable messenger," Gerald handed Levon his visiting card. "That's my address. Material like this always looks more convincing in a newspaper if it is backed up by pictures."

They swept through the first Azerbaijani village at top speed, to the accompaniment of shouts from people standing in the square, and turned off onto the abandoned mountain road. Actually, this narrow path cut out of the mountainside and full of deep ruts could hardly be called a road.

With its engine screaming in protest, the Lada slowly began to overcome the road across the pass. "I shall call my first report 'Three Little Stars'," Gerald thought to himself, his eyes closed. "There were three stars on the labels of the bottle of brandy with which they filled me up, and there were three stars on the shoulder straps of the police officer and the KGB secret agents. Hamlet and Vasili are too young to have ranks above that of senior lieutenant."

Then there was a terrible noise somewhere ahead of them followed by a crash. The car braked violently. Gerald sat up straight in fright. The headlights revealed a pile of still moving stones completely blocking the road. It was a landslide. "We're lucky," said Levon. "It could have landed on us."

It took them about three hours to clear a narrow gap through which the car could pass. They had to drag dozens of boulders aside with a tow rope. They would put the rope around a boulder, hitch the other end on to the car and all together, with their combined efforts, they would move the obstruction aside. "This trip will stay in our memories for a very long time," said Sevda when, with the road clear again, they got back into the car.

"True enough," said Gerald, wiping the sweat from his face with his handkerchief. "On the other hand there will be plenty to tell my readers." And he offered to replace Sevda at the wheel.

But the girl refused. "You are our guest," she said.

Gerald knew already that there was something sacred about the way guests were treated in the Caucasus. So he didn't insist but tried to make himself more comfortable in the back seat and to doze off.

Once again they started the long, tiring climb from one pass to another. Half asleep and rather confused, Gerald had a vision of his parents' home in Nebraska where the honeysuckle was always in bloom outside the window. Then his late mother sitting in her favorite wicker chair on the veranda. And Gerald also saw himself running towards her along the garden path—a little boy with a school satchel on his back.

The first shot that was fired smashed the windshield to smithereens and killed Sevda. With no one to steer it, the automobile crashed into the cliff, then bumped off it and began to roll down the mountain side.

When Gerald came to, everything was quiet and stank of the gasoline that was dripping from a hole in the tank. "Hello!" he cried out hoarsely. "Hello there!"

But Sevda and Levon did not respond.

Gerald tried to raise himself up, but cried out from pain and he again lost consciousness. When he came around later, because of the cold, the night sky was beginning to grow paler in the predawn light. His eyes began to distinguish objects around him. The instrument panel threw a little light on Sevda and Levon in the front seats. They were lying one on top of the other and their faces were black from congealed blood. Gerald realized that they were dead. "My poor friends . . . " he muttered. "I am responsible for your deaths. If I hadn't agreed to drive to Nagorno-Karabakh you would now be sitting at a lecture in your university." Then, trying to ignore the pain, he managed with difficulty to open the car door and tumble out of the wrecked vehicle. It was lying close to a little stream, with its burst radiator jammed into a tree.

Gerald looked about him. All around rose the grim, silent wall of mountain. "Hey!" he shouted. "I am a foreign journalist!" But there was no response. "Who was it that fired at us?" Gerald wondered. The police? The KGB? No. Judging by the noise it made, they had been fired at out of hunting guns by the local inhabitants, although the echo effect in the mountains might have distorted the sound. He tore the sleeve off his shirt and used it to bandage his leg, which was still bleeding. Then, clutching at trees and bushes, he dragged himself up to the road. He found it hard to breathe because his ribs had been bruised by the fall.

Gerald was already in sight of the road when he remembered the exposed films. He would have to go back and take them from Levon's pocket. But he didn't want to even think of doing that because it would mean repeating the climb that had caused him such extreme pain in his injured leg. "To hell with the films!" said Gerald, and he scrambled on further, but stopped after he had gone a few feet. "That would be a rotten trick to play on those young people who have lost their lives. If I don't go and take the films, it would mean their deaths had been pointless. It was precisely for that reason that Sevda and Levon took all the risks. What's more, if I come out of this alive, I'll curse myself for my lack of courage now." And so, hating the world and all that was in it, Gerald turned over with a groan and slid on his back down to the car again.

He reached through the broken window and the found in the pocket of Levon's blood-soaked jacket the film cassettes wrapped in a little plastic bag. He put them in his back pocket.

Once he had recovered his breath, Gerald repeated the climb and finally reached the road. There was still nobody about. It seemed as though they had been fired at by some strange mountain spirits, which had then vanished into thin air and darkness. Just in case, Gerald again cried out for help, but the only reply was a resounding echo. Gerald had no idea what direction to go, but decided to carry on the way they had been headed. Sooner or later he was bound to come across some human habitation.

The sharp pain in his leg had subsided, but his leg had become as heavy as a plank of wood. Gerald took a step and bit his lip. So long as he didn't move, the pain was bearable, but he had only to transfer his weight onto the leg the bullet had struck for his whole body to feel as if it were suffering a thousand sharp pinpricks. And so, getting carefully down on to his knees, Gerald lay down on the dusty, gravely road and crawled. "Oh, no," he thought in a sort of childish puzzlement. "This isn't happening to me. It's somebody else, some stranger who has been injured and is crawling along an abandoned road a night in the wild mountains of the Caucasus. Of course it's not me. After all, I only report events: I don't take part in them."

But there he was. Gerald Jacobson, forty years of age, an American journalist, who had for the first time found out through bitter experience what it meant for one group of people to murder another.

Gerald took a vow: if he survived he would tell the whole Western world the truth—the bitter unadorned truth, with no holds barred, about the tragedy of two peoples set against one another by politics. Because on that day in Yerevan, Levon had been right to recall the words of John Donne: "Do not ask for whom the bell tolls. It tolls for thee."

SIX

The sun had peeped out and then hidden itself again behind dark winter clouds, and the long day of February 27 dragged slowly on, with the evening still ahead.

The neighbors were all still sitting around the funeral table, though all the vodka had been drunk and all the food eaten. The old women in black were nodding from tiredness, and Lyoka was asleep, his head resting on Zeinab's lap. The men were smoking and quietly chatting about life. "There was a lecturer from Moscow who came to talk to us in Afghanistan," Rustam told them. "He told us one very interesting thing. It appears that time stands still. It is we who move."

"Good heavens!" exclaimed Stepa in surprise as beneath the table he stroked one of Aida's knees.

"Nowadays time stands still and we are also marking time in one place," old Aramais commented. "And time is the only thing in the world that, if you lose it, you never get it back."

"How very right you are, Aramais," sighed old Zeinab. "You can lose a great deal of money and still work to get it back again. But our years. . . . There was a time, you know, when I was just twenty-five, like Aida."

Aida took offense and brushed Stepa's hand off her knee. "I'm only twenty-three," she announced.

"She's twenty!" Stepa came heatedly to her support and replaced his hand on her smooth, round knee. "And anyone who argues—I'll fix him!" He glared threateningly.

Rustam winked across to old Aramais—his idea that Stepa should marry Aida had fallen on fertile ground.

Then, with a great deal of noise and shouting, the children returned from school and disappeared into their various houses. By the window opposite the veranda, two big girls from the senior class started up a record player at full blast and began dancing to rock music. "Just look at them!" said Shamanidi in amazement. "What on earth are they doing with their . . . well, their bottoms?"

The girls really were being carried away by the dancing, apparently feeling the wild rhythm of the music in every cell of their strong young bodies. When they noticed that people were watching them they turned the noise down. But before doing so one of them sang through the window:

> *In a forest rose a fir tree,*
> *But who then gave it birth?*
> *Four drunken hedgehogs*
> *And a sober crocodile!*

And, sticking out her tongue, she drew the curtains.

Zeinab shook her head reproachfully. "After all, they know that Alik was buried today, and still they start dancing. Children are growing up with hard hearts."

"There's a time for death and a time for life," Aramais came to their defense, repeating an idea that appealed to him.

"Of course," Rustam gave him a hostile look. "It was an Azerbaijani that died. If it had been an Armenian you wouldn't have said that."

"Why do you say things that are not true?" Aramais said, frowning. "For me there are only two nations in the world, good people and bad people."

"And all Armenians are good," said Farida with a laugh.

"What about Karabakh?" asked Rustam, screwing up his eyes. "Are they the same good Armenians living in Nagorno-Karabakh?"

"There are just as many different kinds as everywhere else." Aramais would not give way.

"Then why do those good Armenians murder the Azerbaijanis there? Why force them to leave the homes their ancestors lived in?"

"Who told you that Armenians are murdering Azerbaijanis?"

"People," Rustam replied. "They escaped from Karabakh and are going around Sumgait telling everyone how badly the Armenians have treated them."

"Can you explain to us, Aramais, why the Armenians behave so badly?" Stepa asked, as he caught the scent of Aida's hair. His eyes clouded over with tenderness.

"I came across those people in the town, and heard what they are saying," said Aramais. "They are lying, just trying to stir up trouble. But I'm not quite sure why."

"They want to start a quarrel," Shamanidi explained.

"That's what it looks like," Aramais agreed.

"That's no good," said Stepa. "What do you think, Aida?"

"Nagorno-Karabakh has belonged to Armenia from ancient times," Shamanidi continued. "The same as Nakhichevan, from which the Azerbaijanis drove the Armenians out and annexed the whole of that territory."

"You're Greek, so shut up," snapped Rustam. "What do you understand about our affairs?"

Shamanidi kept quiet but cast a frightened look at Farida. She replied with an understanding grin that said, "I know, I know."

"Seventy-five percent of the population of Nagorno-Karabakh is Armenian," said Aramais. "So why does the territory have to belong to Azerbaijan?"

Aramais was always upset by this sort of conversation. When the talk came around to the Armenians lands that had been taken by force from Armenia, it always reminded him of his parents and the ghastly slaughter organized by the Turks in 1915. The Turks then put to death, by estimate, a million and a half Armenians. Even the little town in Nakhichevan where Aramais's parents lived did not escape the disaster. Aramais could still recall the crowd of weeping people at the church and the heavily mustached Turkish janissaries on their huge horses. Their bared swords flashed in the sun and blinded you. Aramais, then only three, tried to catch the sun's rays, but his mother held him painfully by the hand and hid him beneath her ample skirt. He could still vaguely recall the long, never-ending path through the mountains along which the Turks drove them. It was dusty and hot, and Aramais was thirsty all the time. Then there was a sort of gap in his memory.

His father told him later that he had even dug a grave to bury him in, but that Aramais suddenly opened his eyes. "He turned out to be a real Armenian," his father joked later. "Everyone thinks that the Armenians have died off, but suddenly we open our eyes again." His mother had died on the way, but his father had succeeded in escaping along with him into Bulgaria. And there he died. He died of nostalgia for his homeland. The doctor could find nothing else wrong with him. He simply got thinner and thinner every day and seemed to become ever smaller, until he turned into a gray-haired child. One day, in early spring, as he lay on his divan, he said: "I am sorry, my son. But I don't want to live any more." He turned his face to the wall and remained silent. When they summoned him to supper he did not reply.

"You must never deprive a man by force of the place where he was born and grew up," Aramais told Rustam. "A man is like a tree—if you cut off his roots he will waste away."

"Let's get this straight." Rustam was not in agreement. "All right, there are more Armenians than Azerbaijanis living in Karabakh, but they made their way into the country in order to squeeze the Azerbaijanis out of it!"

"You're talking a lot of garbage. Do you hear what the fellow is saying?" Aramais pointed to Shamanidi. "Even the Greeks admit it."

Farida burst out laughing, and Shamanidi hung his head guiltily.

"Where is it written down?" said Rustam angrily. "Show me!"

"In all the books you have never read," Aramais cut him off. "Every stone in Nagorno-Karabakh, its crosses and its ancient churches—they all cry to high heaven about it!"

"Tomorrow I will bring you other books from the library in which it is written in black and white that Nagorno-Karabakh always belonged to the Azerbaijanis. They were living there before the Armenians were even called Armenians!"

Old Aramais smiled. "My dear boy," he said, "in literacy alone the Armenians can go back three thousand years."

Rustam was getting really angry now. The fact that Armenian culture went back thousands of years was not disputed even by Azerbaijani historians. "What on earth are you quarreling about, my friends?" said Zeinab. "The land does not belong to either the

Armenians or the Azerbaijanis. The land belongs to Allah. A man is entitled to no more than six feet. As you could see at the cemetery today."

It was the truth, and the contestants stayed silent.

"It's quite possible that I shall soon quit the factory and go to Moscow," Aida announced suddenly.

"What kind of nonsense are you talking now?" said Stepa indignantly. In his mind's eye he already saw Aida as mistress in their own home.

"A girlfriend has written inviting me to go there."

"Your friend's a stupid woman," said Stepa crossly. "I'll write her such a reply that it'll make her mother blush."

"Yes, and who will give her a permit to live in Moscow?" said Farida contemptuously. "And where would she find work?"

"In the Council of Ministers," said Rustam, laughing. "Where else?"

"Why in the Council of Ministers? I'll get a job as a street-cleaner. My friend says that anyone who is willing to become a cleaner gets a room in Moscow immediately and a residence permit in two years."

"I've seen them, those Moscow street-cleaners," Shamanidi intervened. "They're all young girls. They go around in their high heels and expensive coats and keep the roadways clean and tidy. Quite amazing. All day long they are parading themselves in front of the men."

Stepa could just imagine his Aida being inspected through the hungry eyes of the men in the capital. He ground his teeth and muttered something to himself. The neighbors realized that he was cursing someone.

"You're so eager to get away from home," said Aramais to Aida. "Stepa is trying to find a home. It's like on the street—some are rushing in one direction, others are running the other way, and they are all full of worries. They all think that they are the only ones going in the right direction. But in the end they are all gathered together in a quiet spot from which no one can rush away."

Zeinab nodded her head in agreement with what Aramais was saying. The thought of death had recently been occupying her mind more and more. "And we know just how it will end up," said Farida just as contemptuously as before. "She'll come back to Sumgait in a couple of years with her face lined before its time and a child in her arms."

"Very likely," said Zeinab. "Don't be silly, girl." And she spat over her left shoulder, superstitiously.

"What sort of people are you?" Aida asked in a tearful voice. "Never a kind word for anyone."

"You're not the first, and you won't be the last," Farida said, trying to put an end to her dream. "Moscow will chew you up and spit you out again."

"And you!" Aida exclaimed quite illogically, "And you put water in the beer!"

"Prove it!" shouted Farida in reply.

"And you're selling vodka at twenty-five rubles!"

"Prove it!"

"Thief!"

It was quite true that Farida was stealing money in her bar, so she couldn't have such a charge laid against her twice over. Letting out a warlike howl, she grabbed Aida by the hair. Aida gave a penetrating scream. The black-robed women bestirred themselves and ran scared from the veranda.

"You snake!"

"You thief!"

Stepa and Shamanidi rushed to pull apart the two women, who were now fighting in real earnest. Stepa shielded Aida with his body while Shamanidi dragged Farida, still resisting, away from her, for which he received a good kick in the groin. He gasped and, unable to control himself, struck Farida in the face.

"Look what's happening!" Farida shouted at the top of her lungs, for the whole courtyard to hear. "Look, Moslems—an Armenian hitting an Azerbaijani woman!"

Old Aramais shrugged his shoulders in puzzlement. "This Armenian is sitting in his place," he said.

But Shamanidi moved away from Farida in fright. "Shut up, Farida!" he whispered quickly. "Shut up, I'll give you money!"

Farida gave him a good push in the chest with both hands. "I don't need your filthy money!" she said, rolling her eyes madly. "Listen, all of you—he's not Shamanidi—and he's not Greek!"

"Farida!" Shamanidi pleaded with her and extending both hands towards her. "I beg you—please don't!"

"Don't get near me, you bandit!" Farida screamed even louder. "His name is Gevorkyan!"

Shamanidi suddenly dropped onto his knees. "Please, Farida," he said quietly. "I've got a little son growing up now, have a heart."

Windows were being thrown open all over, and the curious faces of neighbors appeared in them. "What do you think you're doing, you bitch, kicking a man when he's down?" said Aramais.

"He escaped from prison and he's living on a false passport."

Shamanidi covered his face with his hands and groaned.

Aramais now understood why Shamanidi had always been so quiet and retiring. "How can you go on living with such a stony heart, woman?" he asked Farida. "How can you look your own son in the eyes?"

"Don't you touch my child!"

"You really are an unfortunate person, Farida," Aramais went on. "When you die there will be nobody to say a kind word at your graveside."

"I shall outlive you, you bloody Armenian!"

Shamanidi rose from his knees. "You will not survive long," he said quietly, taking a knife from his pocket. "I'm going to kill you."

For a moment Farida froze still in fright, eyeing with terror the big switchblade in Shamanidi's hand. Then she started to run away. Shamanidi was about to rush after her, but Rustam and old Aramais got ahold of him, threw him to the ground and took the knife from him.

Shamanidi began to cry. "Now I'm in a mess," he said.

"Have you really escaped from a camp?" asked Rustam.

Shamanidi nodded.

"So!" said Stepa with respect in his voice. "Then escape from here!"

"It's too late. And I'm tired of being on the run."

He got up from the ground, sat on a chair and again took his head in his hands.

"What were you sent down for?" Aramais asked in a rather hostile manner. He didn't like criminals, whether they were Armenians, Russians or Azerbaijanis—it was all the same to him. "I handed over bottles."

"Full ones?" asked Stepa in amazement.

Shamanidi, a nonsmoker, asked for a cigarette and proceeded to tell them his amazing story.

He had been born in a tiny village in the Nagorno-Karabakh region, but later moved to Leninakan. There, he completed seven years at night school and got married. He took a job as a dispatcher in charge of a warehouse belonging to the firm Vtorsyrye. Everywhere he worked he was very soon promoted and put in charge—not of major departments, because his education was not sufficient, but in charge just the same. Shamanidi was an energetic employee, with a good business sense. But no sooner did he get the work going properly than he was warned, "Don't try too hard, smart boy, or you'll find yourself in trouble." The big operators needed a state of confusion—the muddy water in which, as they say, the fish can be caught. If Shamanidi refused to fall in with their ways, they would just squeeze him out of his job "at his own request."

In the beginning he tried to fight the mafia, but one evening he was badly beaten up by a gang of thugs sent for that purpose, and Shamanidi gave up. Along with his wife, he volunteered to go work in the Far North, thinking that in those distant parts where the snow was white and the sea blue, the people would be better behaved. They had not long settled in Petropavlovsk-Kamchatsky before they realized that it was just the same there, only people drank more.

It was in the course of a business trip to the coast of the Sea of Okhotsk that Shamanidi noticed that the settlement he was visiting was literally being buried beneath piles of empty vodka and wine bottles. There were millions and millions of them. Everybody drank—the local native peoples, Koryaks and Chukchis, as well as the Russian men and women. But there was nowhere to return the empty bottles. The local authority issued regulation after regulation demanding that people should not clutter up the sea shore and the streets with empty bottles. But what were people to do with them? You couldn't be expected to carry bottles in a sack to the nearest town, hundreds of miles away.

Shamanidi had an idea. The Petropavlosk-Kamchatsky soft drink factory was at the time out of action. It had run out of containers, that is, those very same empty bottles. There was nothing to put the lemonade and other drinks into. Shamanidi called on the sales department and offered his services. "I don't need any money or anything from you," he said. "Just give me a sheet of your letterhead paper, and a week from now your factory will be working at full speed." The management took him at his word, gave him the paper he asked for, put their official stamp on it, and Shamanidi became an official representative of the factory. Armed with this document, he set out for the port, where he hired a tug and a barge, and a day later arrived back at the settlement. There, he put up prepared notices to the effect that he was ready to receive empty bottles from the population.

In the course of three days, the local children and adults delivered fifty thousand bottles to the barge. That, unfortunately, was all it would hold. A day later Shamanidi, suffering badly from seasickness, arrived with his barge in Petropavlovsk-Kamchatsky. The factory started working at full speed. The manager shook him by the hand to show his gratitude, and even treated him to a glass of brandy.

Shamanidi also did well out of the deal. He paid the people in the settlement ten kopeks a bottle, but sold to the factory at the state price of twenty kopeks. Out of the profits, he had to pay the port for the hire of the tug and the barge, he tipped the sailors generously for helping with loading and unloading, and he was left with a clear three thousand rubles to pocket. When all was said and done he had earned his money honestly: he had rid the settlement of the empty bottles and he had provided the soft drink factory with work. He had benefited everybody. But a week later Shamanidi was summoned to the office of the town prosecutor and arrested on charges of profiteering and swindling. He was sentenced to three years in a prison camp, and the confiscation of all his property. "A year's prison for each thousand rubles," he concluded his story.

"What fucking luck!" said Stepa in amazement, paying no attention to Aida, who had remained very quiet.

In the meantime, Shamanidi's wife had returned to Leninakan, from where, six months later, he received a letter telling him that their long-awaited child had been born. His desire to see his son was so great that Shamanidi couldn't hold out, and he escaped from the prison camp. In Batumi he found a man who sold him a passport that changed him from Gevorkyan to Shamanidi, a Greek.

"And where are your wife and child now?" Rustam asked. Shamanidi did not reply.

"They're very likely also living in Sumgait," Aramais thought to himself, "only in a different district. And they probably see Shamanidi only on Sundays."

"You can spend tonight in my place," Aramais told the unfortunate man. "But tomorrow you'll have to go into hiding."

"Really?" Shamanidi asked hopefully.

"Everything will be all right," old Aramais assured him. "They won't gossip," he added, eyeing the neighbors. Stepa and Rustam nodded in agreement.

"But your room is very small—I'll be in your way."

"I'm on duty tonight." Old Aramais earned a bit of extra money by working as a night guard at the motor tire store. "But tell me—where did Farida get to know about it all?"

"I ran into a guy from our camp in her bar," Shamanidi said reluctantly. "Apparently he told her everything."

At that moment, in great confusion, Farida burst into the courtyard, followed by a young Russian policeman wearing a shoulder belt. "There he is!" Farida pointed her finger at Shamanidi. "An escaped murderer!"

Shamanidi, who had begun to cheer up a little, now collapsed altogether. "So that's that," he said, putting on his hat.

The policeman went up onto the veranda, with Farida following closely behind him for protection. "Sergeant Sementsov." He saluted and put out his hand. "Your passport?"

Shamanidi hastily produced the document. Without bothering to look at it the policeman stuffed it into the pocket of his overcoat. "Come along to the police station with me." Out of prison habit, Shamanidi put his hands behind his back.

"There's no hurry," Aramais intervened. "Sort things out here quietly, in a civilized way. It's a trifling matter. So a couple of neighbors called each other names, said a bit more than they needed to."

"How friendly you make it sound!" Farida butted in. "He threatened to kill me!"

"Just ask the neighbors," Aramais insisted.

"Yes, of course," Zeinab put in her word. "We are telling the truth."

"That woman started it by grabbing me by the hair," said Aida. "She ruined my hairdo."

"She messed up such a beautiful head of hair, the fucking bitch!"

Sementsov gave Stepa a stern glance. "You'll be fined if you use that sort of language."

"He ought to be sent down for ten days too!" Farida shook her fist at Stepa. "He also started waving his fists and using foul language!"

"Shut up!" Rustam barked at her, and then turned to the sergeant. "Listen, friend, let's drop this business . . . "

"I have a written statement from this woman," Sementsov pointed to Farida. "I can see you are back from Afghanistan. I respect you, but we'll sort this out without your help."

"I'm for justice!"

"So just get back into your houses along with your justice." The sergeant laid his hand on Shamanidi's shoulder. "On your way, citizen."

But, having sensed some support for his cause, Shamanidi decided to be difficult. "I'm not going anywhere—sort it out here!"

"You refuse to do as you're told?"

"Yes, I refuse." Shamanidi sat down on the ground.

"Do as you're told, you murderer!" said Farida. "The arm of the law demands it!"

"He's just a kid, not the arm of the law!" Aramais couldn't restrain himself.

The sergeant thought he could lift Shamanidi in one sharp movement and twist his arm behind his back. But although he was of very slight build, Shamanidi turned out to be wiry and strong, and was not to be taken easily. The sergeant realized that he would not be able to cope with Shamanidi on his own, so he summoned a police van on his radio.

While they were waiting for it to arrive, everybody on the veranda stayed silent, estranged from one another. In the end the silence became almost palpable, and unbearable. "I could do with a smoke," said Shamanidi longingly.

"Sit down," ordered the sergeant, undoing his holster.

Aramais rolled a cigarette, lit it and handed it to Shamanidi. "Have a smoke, brother."

Then there was a screech of brakes on the street and a police car drove into the courtyard, a light flashing on its roof. Captain Hussein, an old acquaintance of Aramais, slammed the door and made his way towards the veranda. "So what's the trouble, Sementsov?" the captain asked, surveying the assembled company with a glance. He pretended not to recognize Aramais.

"That one there," whined Farida. "He was going to murder me, an Azerbaijani woman—he threatened me with a big knife!"

"You be quiet, Azerbaijani woman. I'm asking you, Sementsov."

"He's resisting arrest," the sergeant declared.

"Take your hat off," Hussein ordered.

Shamanidi bared his head, to reveal that it had been closely cut, in the prison camp style. "It's clear enough where you have come from," Hussein said.

"Get going!" the sergeant ordered him.

"Don't rush him, Valera," the captain muttered, and with quick, professional movements, he searched Shamanidi and found the switchblade.

"That's it! That's the knife he was going to kill me with!" Farida shouted joyfully.

Hussein cast a reproachful glance at Sementsov, who lowered his eyes guiltily. He had really messed up by not searching the suspect immediately. "Make a note of it all," the captain ordered Sementsov, handing him a notebook. "Who are the witnesses?"

The neighbors hung their heads. "I am a witness," said old Aramais firmly. "Nothing terrible happened, captain. They simply drank a little at the wake and started squabbling."

"One Armenian defending another!" said Farida scornfully. "They always do that."

"You stupid fool," Zeinab hissed at her.

"Are there no more witnesses?"

The neighbors again remained silent. "All right, then," Hussein closed his notebook. "If this fellow has really escaped from a camp, he'll go down for a pretty long stretch. Lead the way, Sementsov."

Using more force than was necessary, the sergeant twisted Shamanidi's arm behind his back and took him to the police wagon.

"Go your ways in peace, citizens," the captain advised them. "Spare your nerves and the nerves of the police too."

Shamanidi turned around as if to say something, but simply shook his head sadly. The sergeant opened the door of the van and pushed him roughly into it.

As he moved away from the veranda into the courtyard, the captain beckoned Aramais, led him aside so that the neighbors couldn't hear, and said quietly: "Don't go into the town today or tomorrow. And don't let your son go either."

"What's happened?" Old Aramais didn't understand.

"Just don't go there," the captain repeated firmly, and left.

The neighbors dispersed gloomily. The only people left on the veranda of poor Alik's house were Zeinab, who was gathering up the dirty dishes and putting them in a basin, and the barmaid Farida.

"So shall I drop in on you this evening to have my fortune told?" Farida asked, as though nothing at all had happened.

"You've done enough fortune telling today," said Zeinab, carrying the basin into the kitchen. "Enough to last you till the end of your days."

Farida snorted and went into her own place, slamming the door noisily behind her.

"What an unsatisfactory day," Aramais thought to himself as he set off for home. It was time to get ready for his job as night watchman.

As he entered his house, a photograph of his late wife Susana immediately caught his eye. Aramais kept it on top of a polished chest intentionally, so that he would always see her face as he came into the room.

No sign of Arshik, of course. "The little devil," Aramais muttered.

He took off his jacket, his tie and his new shoes and chose some more comfortable clothes. He put a rather worn padded jacket on over his shirt, picked up a small-caliber rifle from a corner, and went out. He was allowed to carry a weapon because of his job as a watchman.

It was already quite dark on the street, with just a dim streetlight with one lamp burning at the corner. The dark sky reflected the red of what seemed to be a fire, and there was some strange shouting coming from the center of the town.

"There must be a fire, I suppose," Aramais thought.

The tire warehouse was in the basement of the abandoned school. You entered it by a door strengthened with an iron frame. Aramais unlocked the big padlock and went into the security room. It contained a bare table with a teapot standing on an electric ring and a folding bed with a mattress. He checked the seal on the second door, which also had an iron frame and led directly into the store. Everything was in order. Old Aramais sat down at the table, rolled a cigarette and lit it.

The strange words that the captain of police had uttered came back to him. "What on earth was he trying to warn me about?" Aramais wondered. "He was obviously trying to tell me something important."

Aramais had got to know Hussein when he had been living in exile. As a war veteran, Aramais had had the last two years of his prison sentence commuted to exile in the Khabarovsk region. At that time, now long ago, Lieutenant Hussein had been working as a local policeman in the godforsaken hamlet in which Aramais had been ordered to live. The were on good terms with each other—after all, they were both from the Caucasus.

One day Hussein turned up in full uniform, walking down the snow-lined village street. Aramais was at that moment standing at the partly open window with his face turned to the cold but blindingly brilliant rays of the April sun. He had the feeling that he could already smell the approach of spring, his last spring in exile. The lieutenant turned towards his house. He needed Aramais. The driver of the only truck in the village had fallen sick when out hunting and was now lying in hospital with a high temperature. And Hussein needed urgently to get to Vyselki, another hamlet for which Hussein was responsible as district officer. A woman called Vavilina, who kept the general store there, was robbing and cheating her customers mercilessly.

Hussein didn't know how to drive a car and wanted Aramais to drive him over. Aramais refused, on the grounds that he had not driven practically since the end of the war. But the policeman suddenly pulled out of the pocket of his sheepskin coat a mandarin orange and offered it to Aramais. The sight of that little southern fruit almost brought tears to the old man's eyes: it was like a message from home, from that distant home, so many thousands of miles from that snowbound northern village.

"I received a parcel," said Hussein. "Eat and enjoy it."

Aramais agreed to drive him.

The short winter's day was already coming to an end by the time Hussein had completed his search, drawn up an affidavit and confiscated the fictitious receipts. He put all the papers and the money in the till away in his briefcase, and said to the shopkeeper, "Get your things together, Vavilina, you're coming along with us to the station."

It was getting dark fast. The fog dripped down like condensed milk. With its headlights on full, the truck made its way slowly back to the village. Squeezed between Aramais and the policeman in the driver's cab, Vavilina bumped up and down in silence. Aramais imagined what was ahead for her, felt sorry for her and was angry with himself for getting mixed up in such an affair. In fact, he knew Anya Vavilina, since during his first six months of exile he had taken a room in her big house.

"Go by the Zavalyashka," Hussein ordered him.

Aramais drove as far as the fork and then turned off the road, following a shorter but more dangerous route, along the frozen river Zavalyashka. They had not covered much more than half a mile when the ice cracked beneath them with a frightening noise, the truck slid over on to its side and they landed in icy water.

Aramais scrambled out of the cab and felt for the bottom of the river with his feet. The dark water, mixed with floating pieces of ice, reached up to his waist. The Zavalyashka was a shallow river. Aramais forced the other door open and helped Anya and the furiously cursing policeman to get out. Hacking their way through the ice they managed to get themselves to the river bank, but then they were seized by a cold that seemed to go right through them. Aramais's padded jacket and trousers were stiff with ice and had become unbelievably heavy. Their feet and legs were quickly frozen, and they could feel nothing with their fingers. The worst off was the policeman, who had fallen into the water right up to his head and had lost his uniform cap. His hair stood up in icy clumps.

Aramais could not remember how they managed to get to Posyolka. He kept falling, then getting up again, crawling on all fours through the snowdrifts and, along with Anya, almost at the end of their strength, dragging Hussein who was fast losing consciousness. Aramais recovered in Anya's house. His body felt as though he had hundreds of needles sticking into it. He lay back, then woke up, quite naked, with Anya Vavilina's flushed red face peering down at him.

"What are you doing here?" he asked, still not realizing properly where he was and amazed to find his voice so weak.

"Lie still!" said Anya, breathing heavily and fiercely rubbing Aramais's hairy chest.

"Where's Hussein?"

"He's sleeping next to you, your precious Hussein," said Anya. "I've rubbed him all with spirit, too—wrapped him in a blanket. What a pity it is my man is off hunting in the forest, he would have melted down some bear fat for you."

Aramais was about to ask something else, but fell again into a deep sleep. When he opened his eyes in the morning the first thing he saw was ruble notes, all crumpled up with wetness, the search warrant and the fictitious receipts hanging all around the room. They were being dried out, clipped to a line with clothespin. Beside the next bed, on which a thoughtful policeman was sitting in his underwear, there was a table. On it lay his briefcase, and his gun in a holster. Anya was not in the room.

"What are you going to do now, Hussein?" Aramais asked quietly.

The policeman said nothing.

Still feeling rather weak, Aramais stood up, took his clothes, now almost dry, from the stove and began to dress.

"She saved my life," Hussein said at last.

"And what about you?"

"I'm supposed to put her inside."

"If you do that, how will you ever be able to look your child in the eyes again?"

"I don't know." Hussein looked around the room, at the bed on which he had been tossing about in feverish delirium, then the badly whitewashed stove with its pile of chopped wood, the bucket used as a washbasin, the brightly colored curtains in the frozen window, and he repeated, "I don't know."

"Burn the warrant, the receipts and your briefcase," Aramais said. "The money you can hide under a mattress—she'll find it later. Back at the station you can say that everything fell into the river and was lost." Aramais turned and left the room.

The policeman did just what Aramais suggested. The inquiry into the affair dragged on for a couple of weeks. Aramais was called in for questioning, and he confirmed the policeman's story. Finally they wound the case up. Vavilina was fired from the shop, and Hussein was given a severe reprimand for having lost material evidence.

Many years later, a trick of fate brought them together again, but this time in Sumgait. They ran into each other one Sunday in Farida's bar, the cultural center for the whole of the southern part of the town. They were both delighted to meet again, just like old friends. They went to Aramais's house, drank some wine, recalled people they had known in the north and the search at Anya Vavilina's, and had a good laugh.

"If Hussein is still only a captain," Aramais reflected as he sat at the table in the security room, "that means he has preserved something human in his policeman's heart. And if that's the case, I shall have to go and buy a bottle of good brandy tomorrow and call on him at home. Perhaps we can think up something together to help poor Shamanidi."

SEVEN

T he building Bella lived in was not far from the market. It was a multistory colossus of yellow brick, which towered above the five-story blocks around it like a visitor from the city among poor relatives. There were several buildings like it scattered around the town. The inhabitants of Sumgait called them the "houses of gentlefolk," after Turgenev's phrase, because that was where the Party and government elite lived. Bella's father had been accorded the honor of a three-roomed flat in that building because he was considered to be one of the best surgeons in Azerbaijan.

Arshik was going to call on Bella for the first time, and was rather embarrassed when he tromped on the well-polished parquet floor in the hallway. "Should I take my shoes off?" he asked, for some reason in a whisper, when Bella opened the door to him.

She laughed. "Drop your middle-class manners and step this way!"

In the living room, which had lots of comfortable furniture and many bookcases, Arshik was greeted by Bella's father, a tall and well-built man of about forty-five, in a cheerful, easy-going manner. He patted Arshik on the back and asked where he had got to know his daughter. Arshik explained that they had studied together in school, right from the first class.

"That means you two have a lot to talk about," her father said with a wink. "Do you drink wine?"

Arshik answered that he didn't drink wine, though he had tried it more than once.

"You don't shoot drugs?" Her father was joking, but there was a note of concern in his voice. As a doctor he knew how widespread drug-taking was in the town, especially among the young people.

"No," said Arshik, now beginning to be offended.

"And you don't smoke hashish?" asked the man, feigning surprise.

"I don't smoke at all," Arshik said with a frown.

"Heavens, that's a weight off my mind!" said Bella's father. "A boyfriend like that is worth a million dollars!"

"Daddy!" said Bella, blushing.

"Why? Isn't that the truth?" her father said teasingly. "You don't come across in the present generation of young people many young men with such qualities. Look—he's even wearing a tie!"

"If you've made up your mind to make fun all the time, Arshik and I will go to the movies." Bella was offended and Arshik silently supported her.

Her father surrendered, raising both hands above his head. "All right, I won't do it anymore. Bring our dear Arshik some tea, and with your permission I'll drink a glass of brandy."

Over tea, the conversation touched on the events in Nagorno-Karabakh, and the meetings in Sumgait. Arshik blurted out that he didn't care much what country Nagorno-Karabakh belonged to, Armenia or Azerbaijan. But if they had decided to attach the region to the state of New York, he would have gone off that very evening and fought to the last drop of his blood.

Bella's father gave a snort and studied the boy with real curiosity. But his words provoked Bella to protest. "It was people like you who in 1915 let the Turks slaughter half our people!" she exclaimed.

Arshik, too, had never been able to understand how Armenian men had been able to permit the Turks to organize such a blood bath. Why had they not taken up arms and defended their families? "If anyone were to come in here now," he said heatedly, "and start to insult us, I would tear him to pieces with my bare teeth!"

Bella looked at him with admiration, and Arshik noticed her reaction with satisfaction. "They were tricked," Bella's father explained, and he proceeded to tell the story of what actually happened.

In 1915, Turkey was preparing to take part in the First World War, on Germany's side. It seemed quite natural to the Armenians then living in Turkey that their men should be called to military service. They were regarded as citizens of the Ottoman empire. The procedure was usually as follows: An officer of the Turkish army would arrive in some little Armenian town or settlement, bring together the recruits on his list and take them to a central point. But on the way, usually somewhere in the mountains, still without weapons, the recruits would find themselves ambushed. They would be shot by machine-gun fire, and those who were only wounded would be finished off with a bayonet. That was how tens of thousands of the youngest and toughest Armenian men met their ends. This carefully planned annihilation of Armenians went on for a whole year. And it was only when they had finished with the men that they embarked on a general massacre. They then set about butchering everybody one after the other—women, old people and children.

"Didn't the Armenians guess that the men were being killed? I can't believe it!" cried Bella.

"After all," Arshik agreed, "it went on for a whole year."

Bella's father sighed. "The dead tell no tales. It's true, there were plenty of rumors. But they were so monstrous that people refused to believe them. People just couldn't take it in. Such a terrible thing might take place during the Mongol invasion or in the Middle Ages. But for it to happen in our enlightened age! No, they just couldn't believe it, my grandfather told me.

"After all, the people who did it, the Turks, lived side by side with them—their houses were just on the other side of the garden hedge. Together with the Armenians, they toiled in the fields, trampled the ripe grapes in the autumn and drank the new wine at the same table. Their children went to school along with the Armenian children. . . . But let's drop this conversation." Bella's father shook his head as though driving away some terrible sights seen in the past.

"I swear!" Bella raised her hand. "I swear I will give birth to a son and he will avenge us for all our sufferings!"

Now it was Arshik's turn to stare at her in admiration.

"Now, in order to give birth," her father commented, "you have to get married, at the very least." He smiled. "I say that with authority, as a doctor."

"Only not to your Rafik," Bella said with a snort.

Arshik's ears pricked up. The appearance of some Rafik on the horizon was not to his liking. "He's a decent young man from a good

Armenian family," her father countered. "He promises to become a good doctor."

"He's sort of a chicken."

This made her father angry. "What nasty language for a young girl to use!"

"Whenever I see him it seems to me that all the Armenians in the world gathered up all of their fear of life and handed it over to him!"

"Seems you've had it, Rafik," Arshik thought to himself. "But I'll punch your face in when I see you, all the same."

"Rafik is no coward, but a well brought up boy with very gentle ways." Bella's father turned to Arshik for support. "Is there anything wrong in that?"

In reply Arshik mumbled something indistinguishable while at the same time repeating to himself his decision to beat up Rafik in the near future.

"That's the sort of husband all the women dream of!" said Bella with a laugh.

"You're a stubborn little ass," said her father with a wave of his hand. "I'm tired of your disagreeable character. Would you care for some more tea?" he asked, turning to Arshik.

Arshik refused, scowling. He was upset because Bella's father had started discussing Rafik in his presence. "The Armenians of Sumgait are really out of luck," said the doctor. "The lovely Bella will not give her beautiful hand to any one of you. Only General Andronik would be worthy of her."

"And I still maintain that your Rafik is a coward!"

"Has he ever allowed anyone to offend you?" asked Arshik hopefully. "You only have to tell me and I'll fix him."

"Just let someone try and offend me!" said Bella aggressively. "But it's something else that I'm trying to explain to my father. His Rafik Melkonyan is simply afraid to open his mouth about anything. Anybody can walk all over him like on a doormat."

"What on earth is this girl saying?" her father said indignantly.

"I know him better than you do! I've even kissed him!"

Arshik gave Bella such a look that she quieted down.

Her father laughed. "You say Rafik is afraid of everything," he said. "But to kiss such a wild animal must be like going into the cage with a tiger!"

"But before kissing me he repeated a dozen times over that he was determined to marry me!" Bella said this deliberately to annoy Arshik.

Hurt by her treachery, Arshik was about to get up and leave, but he held back. He didn't want Bella's father to think, "There you are—son of a shoemaker and badly brought up."

"Just listen to me, father," said Bella. "I don't want to have children by types like that. They grow up to be frightened people. The sort of people that anybody can hurl an insult at and they don't react at all. They don't react because they are forced to live outside their own native land."

"Oh, yes? And what's it like in Armenia itself?" her father objected. "Do you think they all live like brothers there? Nothing of the sort. Armenia is a small country where everyone thinks he is an important person, with the result that they are always clashing with each other. And they get hurt, as I know only too well."

"I'm talking about something different," said Bella, unwilling to give in. "Your Rafik has an inborn readiness to be submissive."

"It's not fair to discuss a fellow's character in his absence."

"Rafik himself admits it! He's even got a theory about it. He reckons that we Armenians can survive in this world only on one condition—by making ourselves invisible! Everywhere—not just in the Soviet Union, but in France, America, Syria. As though we didn't exist, as though we were the same as they!"

Her father shrugged his shoulders. "Well, you have to sing the songs that are being sung around you. That's how life is, not only for the Armenians."

"I agree, you can sing along with the others. But with one's own voice, one's own!"

"That's just nationalistic raving," her father cut her off. "Have we really suffered so little from Turkish, Persian, and now Azerbaijani nationalists that we want to get mixed up in the filth ourselves? It's a different matter when it comes to preserving one's own language and one's own traditions—"

"One's own dignity!" Bella broke in. "Dignity!"

"Armenians, Turks, Germans . . . " said her father thoughtfully. "I know only one thing—be kind, live an honest life, do your work well, and then you will preserve your dignity and others will behave to you in the same way."

The telephone rang in his study and he left the room. "What are you sulking about?" Bella inquired, laughing. In bitter words Arshik told her all he was thinking about her behavior and the cowardly Rafik she had allowed to kiss her.

Bella did not have time to reply. Her father came out of his study, his face as white as a sheet. "What's the matter with you?" she asked in alarm. "Is it your heart?" Her father did not reply. "Daddy, do you hear me?"

Her father looked at her absently and then grinned sadly. "It's a footnote to our conversation. A former patient of mine phoned to say that I should get out of town immediately, along with my family."

"Why?" asked Bella in amazement.

"There's going to be a massacre. The Azerbaijanis are going to slaughter the Armenians."

"What garbage!" said Bella indignantly. Arshik couldn't believe it either.

"No, children, it's not garbage," the doctor said with a sigh. "The man who phoned works in a very serious organization. Knowing everything is part of their official duties."

"Perhaps they're just trying to scare us?" Arshik suggested.

"Unfortunately it is true," said the doctor, and proceeded to explain. "The man who phoned is not likely to mislead me. Three months ago I performed a very complicated operation on him—you could even say I saved his life. And it is out of gratitude that he has warned me. He gave the warning and immediately hung up on me, as though he were afraid of something himself."

"This madness just doesn't make any sense to me," Bella said, adding confusedly, "What are we going to do now?"

"I don't know," said her father, as he looked out of the window, his dark eyes filled with sadness. The three of them remained silent.

"No, things can't be left like that!" the doctor suddenly declared, determination in his voice. "We can't permit these thugs to spill human blood!"

He went off into the next room, to return soon after in a suit, the jacket of which was covered with all kinds of decorations. Among them was the highest Soviet decoration—the Order of Lenin. "Where are you going, Daddy?" asked Bella in surprise. Her father usually dressed up only on special ceremonial occasions.

"To the town committee of the Party. They must be warned." Then suddenly he remembered that he had not taken his Party card with him, without which he would not be allowed into the town committee building. Arshik watched the doctor go into the study, his medals clinking, take from the drawer of his desk a red folder with the same profile of Lenin on the cover, study it for a moment and then put it away carefully in the inside pocket of his jacket.

"There's something else you can do," the doctor told his daughter, as he left the study and wiped his forehead with the palm of his hand. "On the desk in there you will find my notebook. Find in it the names of all the Armenians and warn them of the massacre that's being prepared."

"Very well, father."

"Try not to go into details—just warn them and leave it at that. They ought to get themselves out of town for awhile. In fact, each one will have to decide for himself where best to hide his children. And you, young man," he turned to Arshik. "Won't you keep me company?"

Arshik didn't understand. "The fact is, I need a witness in case I am kept there," the older man said with a wry grin. "There have been cases where people went into the town committee building and nobody ever saw them again."

"Of course I'll go with you," Arshik said eagerly.

"You're not afraid?"

Arshik gave him such a look that he had to apologize, and in a friendly way he mussed up Arshik's hair.

"Daddy!" Bella cried out when her father reached the door on to the street. He stopped. "I love you and I'm proud of you."

"Now, now—no fine speeches," the doctor said in some embarrassment, and off he went, with Arshik beside him.

The doctor drove slowly, although there was practically no traffic. He steered his Boya carefully through a group of people who were walking right in the middle of the road, heading for the square where meetings were held and the Sumgait town Party committee had its headquarters.

As they drove along, people stared with curiosity into the car and banged on the roof with their hands. Arshik was eager to jump out and punish the offenders but the doctor would not let him. On the whole the people were not being especially aggressive. There was only one elderly Azerbaijani with a long mustache who, when he saw the decorations on the doctor's jacket, hissed through his teeth, "Just look what a lot of pretty toys he's got!"

Bella's father gritted his teeth but said nothing.

It proved impossible to drive right up to the committee building. All access to it was blocked by buses. Like lumbering elephants, they were parked all across the street, with police reinforcements beside them. Bella's father left his car at the roadside. "We'll do the rest on foot."

"I know the way," Arshik said.

He led the doctor through the side streets and courtyards he knew so well and brought them right to the main Party building in Sumgait, with its heavy, gray facade. In architecture and color, this temple to the new religion known as Communism was an exact copy of all the other buildings belonging to the city and district Party committees, which held the whole country in their grip, from the Pacific Ocean to the Caspian Sea.

There were even bigger crowds of police here, and there were secret police walking up and down in civilian clothes with sharp, flashing eyes. "Where are you going?" demanded a police officer with a major's shoulder straps, blocking their way. A man in a raincoat immediately popped up beside him. He kept his hands in his pockets, where he no doubt had a gun.

"My name is Mesropyan." Bella's father showed his Party card to the major. "I need to see the secretary of the city committee, as a matter of extreme urgency." The major took the Party card, spent a long time comparing the photograph with the person, flicked through the pages to make sure the contributions had been paid (it was a strictly observed rule that you could not enter any Party office unless all dues had been paid) and then handed the Party card over to the man in civilian clothes. He in turn also went through the pages, and then inquired, "What is your business?"

"Party business, state business," said the doctor firmly.

"I'll find out." The man in the raincoat turned away and whispered something into his crackling pocket radio telephone. Apparently having obtained permission, he nodded to the major.

"You can go in," said the major.

Arshik took this to mean that he was permitted to enter as well, but they stopped him. "And who is this young man?"

"My daughter's fiance," the doctor said, to Arshik's surprise.

"The fiance will wait here."

Arshik looked inquiringly at Bella's father. For just a moment there was a hint of fear in the older man's eyes, but he took control of himself, gave Arshik a reassuring sign and began to climb the wide steps up to the committee headquarters.

In the entrance hall he was again stopped by a policeman in civilian clothes. "Name?"

"Mesropyan."

"Check it," the agent ordered the cop sitting at the small table beside him. He checked a list and said: "Mesropyan is OK."

"Second floor. Reception area for the First Secretary."

The doctor climbed up the carpeted stairway to the second floor, then walked down a long corridor, past a row of polished doors, knocked on the door of the First Secretary's waiting room, and then walked in.

A rather plump man in a finely tailored blue suit rose to meet him. Beyond his desk was another door marked "First Secretary." The man introduced himself as the duty officer, but did not offer to shake hands or invite the doctor to sit down. His eyes were expressionless and his eyelids swollen. "Kidney trouble," the doctor diagnosed the problem automatically to himself as he made his introductions.

"What can I do for you?"

"I must talk to the secretary," said the doctor, rather agitated. "With the First Secretary. On a very important matter."

"It's Saturday today—not a working day. The Secretary is resting."

"With such a tense situation in the town and he's resting!"

"The First Secretary is also a human being and has the right to the time off guaranteed by the constitution. Tell me what your business is."

"The constitution also guarantees citizens the right to defend the state!"

"What do you have in mind?"

"Don't you ever go outside onto the street?" Bella's father burst out. "Look what's going on in the town!"

"No need to shout. I hear very well."

"Shouting's not enough—the church bells should be ringing out!" The doctor was shaken by the total indifference of this Party boss, who merely shrugged his shoulders.

"Yes, the people are holding meetings. But they have every right to voice their opinions on all the questions that worry them, including the question of Nagorno-Karabakh. There's no need to get upset, comrade Mesropyan. I gather that the same thing is happening in Yerevan."

"I'm not talking about Nagorno-Karabakh!"

"Excuse me, I hadn't finished. You, the intelligentsia, have always been demanding that the Party allow for a variety of opinions. Now you've got it. So your pretensions are without foundations. Especially since we have the situation in the town under control."

"I did not come here to talk about Karabakh, but about the fact that a massacre of people of Armenian nationality is being prepared in the town!"

"Where do you get such information from?"

"Don't you have the same information?"

"It's all idle gossip. Just rumors going around the bazaar. Rumors like that are being put around deliberately by the enemies of *Perestroika* to discredit the democratic developments now taking place in our society."

"Listen." The doctor tried to get a grip on himself. "I've been a member of the Party for twenty years, I'm a medical doctor and I'm in charge of a surgical department. You can see the awards by which the government has recognized the honest work I've done." The official's face remained devoid of expression. "Do I have the right to see the First Secretary or not?"

"Why do you not want to deal with me?"

"My information is of a confidential nature. I can entrust it only to the First Secretary."

"It's his day off."

"Give me his address—I'll go and call on him."

"I'm not allowed to do that."

"Then what about his home telephone number?"

"That's also forbidden."

Bella's father just couldn't make out what sort of a person he was talking to—an Azerbaijani, a Russian or an Armenian. The town Party's duty officer had such a characterless, standard face and way of behaving. He was the typical middle-level Party official you could meet throughout the country. "Are you a robot or a real person?"

"Don't forget where you are."

The doctor held his tongue. "Yes," he said. "Now at last I have understood where I am."

"What do you mean?" asked the official quickly, and for the first time in the course of the conversation his slightly swollen eyes showed some signs of interest.

"What you yourselves know perfectly well," said the doctor earnestly.

"I would like to hear exactly what you mean by those words," asked the official in an insinuating tone. His indifference had disappeared and he had begun to look like a hunting dog that had hit on a fresh scent.

The doctor did not have time to reply. A well-dressed man, who unknown to the doctor was the famous journalist from Moscow, floated grandly into the waiting room, still in his short jacket. With a friendly nod to the official, he went straight into the First Secretary's office. After he had shut the door behind him, a man's voice could be heard welcoming him.

"The Secretary's in his office!" said the doctor. "You have been lying to me!"

He moved in the direction of the office, but the official had pressed some knob on his desk, moved quickly ahead of him and closed the door with the notice on it. At the same moment a camouflaged door built into the oak paneling of the reception room burst open and two stocky police agents stepped out of it. One of them aimed a revolver at Bella's father while the other pushed him up against the wall, skillfully searched him, twisted his arm behind his back and looked at the official.

"Take him away," he said.

The doctor put up no resistance. He realized he was up against a concrete wall. When they had marched him out of the reception room, the official called out to him ominously, "I'll make a note of your name, Mesropyan." And, leaning over his desk, he jotted something down in a notebook and underlined it twice.

The agents escorted Bella's father down the corridor, almost at a run, and took him down to the exit. At the main door they even straightened up his tie and stuffed his shirt back into his pants. Then, with a gentle push on the back, they put him outside.

People were still arriving in the square. Bella's father looked at them and went to the bottom of the steps, where he found Arshik still waiting at the police barrier. He had such a look on his face that Arshik did not dare to inquire about the result of the meeting in the town committee. They set off silently to find the car.

Before switching on the engine, Bella's father took his Party card out of his pocket. With a sort of strange grin, he studied it, with its profile of Lenin looking inspired and reaching for the future. Then, with his steady surgeon's fingers, he tore it up and threw it out of the car.

A very worried Bella was waiting for them at home. "So what happened at the town committee?" she demanded of her father.

"Did you warn the other people?"

"Yes, I did."

"Then get together all the most essential things. We are going to get out of town."

Bella understood. "That means it's true?"

"Please don't ask me any unnecessary questions," her father said irritably and went into his study.

Without saying anything to Arshik, Bella went off to gather things together. He was left cooling his heels in the hallway.

Arshik overheard Bella's father talking by telephone to his wife, who was in Baku attending a pediatricians' conference, insisting that she delay her return to Sumgait.

"Why is he making such a big deal?" Arshik wondered, rather condescendingly. "There isn't going to be any pogrom. They'll make a lot of noise on the square, drink some wine, and towards evening they'll go back home. Is he scared?"

Bella's father then placed an urgent call to Yerevan, and asked the operator to connect him with the Armenian government office. "Hello, hello!" he shouted into the receiver. "Is that Yerevan? What the devil . . . Hello?"

The phone fell silent. He was cut off.

Arshik then, through the open door of the study, saw Bella's father leave the telephone, sit at his desk, and clutch his head with his hands. Arshik pulled the unaccustomed tie from his neck, quietly opened the street door and left the house.

He stopped at the entrance to the building and waited a little, hoping that Bella would realize what had happened and would come running after him. But there were no signs of her, and Arshik, offended, set off for the market in search of the man who had promised to get him some metal tips for boots.

The market was close by. Arshik usually hurried through it, but today there was something he didn't like about the usual bustle, although in some ways everything was as usual—customers with their baskets were strolling along between the stalls, checking the prices, bargaining with eastern temperament, while in the traditional manner the unshaven traders were grabbing at people's clothes, offering winter saffron apples and orange persimmons.

Arshik had an internal seismograph that told him the people doing business were all Azerbaijanis. There were no Armenians from the outlying villages standing at their stalls. He was surprised, but didn't attach any special importance to the fact.

Arshik was not a nationalist, although he often got into fights when he was given the humiliating label of "Armyashka." He was just as unexcited by the problem of Nagorno-Karabakh as by the noisy meetings being held by Azerbaijanis on the streets of Sumgait. He was of course more in sympathy with the Armenians of Karabakh, but what Arshik wanted most of all was for nobody to prevent him from taking care of his own business. He was of course upset by the continual difficulties that arose in his relations with the Azerbaijanis he knew. When a conflict arose it was always clear that Arshik was an outsider among them and that he was there on sufferance. But even on the surface Arshik was very little different from them: he spoke excellent Azerbaijani and knew the local customs.

The experience of this biased attitude developed in him a keen sense of distrust towards everything around him. It had developed back in his childhood, in that same market, where life had taught him his first lesson.

In those days old Aramais used to drive to market every Saturday to sell the sandals he had made at home. Susana had already died and, so the boy should not be left alone, he took Arshik along with him. At the end of every such excursion Aramais used to give the boy a few rubles to spend on children's treats—ice cream or turkish delight. But Arshik did not spend the money. He was saving it up to buy a bicycle. This was a little secret of his that no one else was allowed to know. The idea was that one fine day he would appear on the street, riding a bicycle shining with chrome, and surprise the other boys in the district.

One day Arshik decided to exchange the coins he had collected for a single large bill. While Aramais was busy selling sandals Arshik embarked on his first independent deal. He picked out from among the dense crowd in the market a man who seemed to him to be worthy of his trust—white suit, cane and a kindly look in his eyes. Arshik went up to him and asked politely if he would help him to exchange the cash he had in a little box for a twenty-five ruble note.

The man wondered whether Arshik was out to trick him. Did the box really contain twenty-five rubles? Arshik offered to let him open the box and count the money. The man took the metal box from him and weighed it in his hand. "Yes," he agreed, "There probably is twenty-five rubles here." Then, after stuffing the box into his pocket, he moved off unhurriedly through the market.

Arshik, quite shocked, caught up with him and tugged at his sleeve, saying, "Mister, you forgot to give me my note for twenty-five rubles."

The man stopped and asked in a kindly manner, "What are you talking about, boy?"

Arshik began patiently to explain that he had given him a box containing twenty-five rubles in small change. The man heard him out, shrugged his shoulders in puzzlement and said, "You've probably had too much sun. Go sit in the shade by the fence." And, waving his stick, he went on his way. Arshik ran after him again, clutching at his white trousers, then burst into tears and begged the man to return his box. A crowd of curious onlookers gathered around, but they couldn't understand what was going on. A small boy was shouting, hanging on to the leg of a well-dressed person and crying.

Then a policeman appeared on the scene. "What's all the noise about?" he inquired.

The man in the white suit explained calmly and politely that this was some street boy who was pestering him and demanding twenty-five rubles.

"Yes," Arshik cried out. "He took twenty-five rubles off me and won't give them back!"

At which the man turned to the crowd, saying: "Now judge for yourselves, folk, and you too, officer, where could such a small boy get hold of a sum like twenty-five rubles?" At this point the crowd and the policeman tsk-tsk'd in agreement, nodded to one another, and began to abuse Arshik. The policeman pulled him off the man, twisted his ear till it hurt, and dragged him off to the police station. But the man stopped him, pushed a couple of rubles into the policeman's hand and asked him to let Arshik go. Then he walked off, having patted Arshik paternally on the head. The policeman released Arshik and told him he should thank Allah that he had come across such a kind man.

This incident had left a deep impression in the child's memory. Having grown up with a heart embittered from an early age and distrustful of everybody, Arshik was left with only one little corner that was untouched—his love for his adopted father, old Aramais. He was the only person he trusted. Now, years later, he was again saving up, again secretly, both the money he earned by honest work and what he got by other means, in order to give his father an unexpected present in his old age. Arshik had long dreamed of taking old Aramais to Armenia, putting him into a luxury room in Yerevan's best hotel, and visiting with him the church of Gegart.

Arshik could hear shouting coming from the direction of the market entrance. He decided to go see what was going on. Right by the gateway there was a shell game, locally called "Hunt the Boy," going on. Surrounded by a crowd of curious onlookers, the trickster, Dias Ismailov, was squatting, moving the little ball about with deft movements of his hands, covering it up with first one and then another metal thimble. Arshik knew how it was done. The only people who didn't know were the folk up from the country who dared to pit themselves against Ismailov. They never guessed that Ismailov had another little ball hidden behind an especially long nail on his middle finger. That was why it was practically impossible to win against Ismailov. At the right moment, he could choose to put the little ball beneath either of the two thimbles.

Ismailov had two assistants moving about among the uninitiated visitors from village and town. Pushing each other excitedly aside, they would throw their money into the kitty, practically always winning, then they would go away and return later to have another bet, until somebody from among the trusting spectators made up his mind to join in the game, too. Five minutes later they would have squeezed out of him all the money he had earned in a week's trading in the market.

Ismailov caught sight of Arshik and told him that Jafarov would come in an hour. Yavor Jafarov was the man who smuggled soles for boots out of the factory and, when the occasion arose, he could even bring out a whole roll of leather, which was in even shorter supply.

Arshik was not inclined to go back home and sit around at the dreary wake. So he bought himself a cup of roasted pumpkin seeds and leaned up against the fence, casually spitting out the husks. As he waited for

Jafarov, he watched the people passing by. He had always liked the hustle and bustle of the market. It seemed to be something apart from the ordinary, with something of a holiday atmosphere. Every kind of situation to be met with in life cropped up here, only to break up again at once: the cunning and the trusting, the greedy and the generous met there. In a very short time someone made himself rich, while someone else lost all his money. The market was the place where you could at the same time see and buy everything the earth produced and human hands created. "The market and the cemetery," old Aramais had once told him, "they are the face of every town and people. If you want to know what sort of people live there just have a look at those two places and you'll understand at once."

Amongst the crowd streaming out of the gates to the market, Arshik suddenly caught sight of a tall girl with a dark complexion and a very purposeful gait. She was obviously looking for someone. Arshik's heart beat faster at seeing her. It was Bella.

He detached himself from the fence and straightened up. There were two things in life that embarrassed Arshik: that he was so short and that his nose had been broken in a fight. It was especially his height that bothered him, though, when he was strolling with Bella down the main street of the town.

"How did you find me?" he asked as he strode across to meet her.

"Aramais told me."

Arshik realized that Bella had had time to go to his house. He wondered whether his father had taken to her or not.

Bella took him by the hand, led him across to a closed market stall, and there looked him straight in the eyes. "What's happened?" asked Arshik, rather confused. "Why didn't you get out of town?"

"My father was called to the hospital to perform an operation."

"A fine time for that!" said Arshik crossly.

"It was a very urgent case. Some journalist was brought from Baku in a helicopter. They found him lying wounded in the mountains."

"Couldn't they have done the operation there?"

"They were afraid—he was a foreigner, after all. He was beginning to get gangrene. My father locked me in the house and went off to do the operation."

"How did you get out?"

"By the neighbor's balcony. I left my father a note that I would be back soon and ran off."

"So," Arshik thought to himself happily, "she loves me!"

But at this point Bella asked him very seriously, still looking him straight in the eyes, "Are you Armenian?"

"As if you didn't know."

"Yes or no?"

"Of course I'm Armenian."

"Then you are obliged to help me."

"For you, like a young Communist, I'm always ready!" Arshik joked, rather disappointed. He had hoped that Bella had escaped from her home just to see him.

"Not for me," Bella corrected him. "For your fellow countrymen."

Arshik looked around him. Nobody was paying any attention to them: people were still hurrying into the Saturday market and there was no hint that somebody amongst them was preparing to slaughter Armenians. "What can I do to help?" he asked. Arshik was happy all the same that they had made it up in such a natural way and that it would now be possible to agree on a meeting the next day. The disco in the park was open on Sundays.

"I have phoned around to all the Armenians we know. But there are seven addresses left. They are people without a telephone. I will deal with four of them and you will warn the others about the pogrom, okay?" Bella took out a sheet of paper with addresses on it and divided it into two parts. "There you are, look . . . the Tumanyans on the embankment. The Sarkisovs in Post Office Lane, and there in their own house, number seventeen, live the Bablumyans."

"A man promised to bring me some soles for boots," Arshik said awkwardly. "Is it okay if I go to these people in half an hour?"

Bella's eyes flashed in anger. "How can you be bothering about boots now?"

"Okay, I get it," Arshik quickly agreed, and offered gallantly, "Give me four addresses and leave three for yourself."

Bella and Arshik exchanged their lists of names. "As soon as you've seen these people come back here to the market. I'll wait for you at the bus stop. But if you get back first," Bella instructed him, "then you must wait for me."

"I'm ready to wait for you to the end of my life!" Arshik said with real feeling and took Bella by her hand, which was small and warm.

"We'll meet up and go right to your father. We'll get him to join us and set off for the country from our house."

"So let's get going," said Arshik in a businesslike way. The first people he decided to warn were the Oganyans. They lived further away than anyone, on the street named after "Twenty-six Baku Commissars."

As Arshik made his way through the town, he felt great respect for Bella. Her father was probably at home going out of his mind with worry, while she was chasing around the whole of that dangerous town on her own. What would happen if the Azerbaijanis went wild? They had, of course, never been very fond of the Armenians, but to go so far as to organize a pogrom?

Arshik had been made to realize for the first time that he was not like the people around him when he was a child. It happened in the summer, the first summer after Aramais took him from the children's home. Arshik was about seven at the time. He used to play in the courtyard with Alik Beibutov at the game of "nozhicki" ("knives"). They would draw a circle on the damp earth and take turns throwing a penknife into it from various positions—sitting, standing, from the shoulder— and so divide up the circular area into parts. The winner was the one who seized most of the ground inside the circle. In the course of a game Arshik told Alik Beibutov a frightful story about a doctor who had committed murders. He had overheard old Zeinab telling the story to the old women.

The doctor, a handsome fellow of about thirty, had traveled around the whole country marrying old but wealthy women. A month after marrying him, they all died of a heart attack. After which the handsome doctor would sell up their belongings, gather up any valuables and go to another town, where he would get married again. In this way he eventually reached Sumgait. There he married an acquaintance of Zeinab's, a childless widow of a dentist. He had left her in his will his own brick-built house, a car and a whole jar of gold hidden in the ground in the yard. After the marriage of the handsome doctor and the widow, the neighbors often heard wild laughter in their house at night, and within a week she too had died of a heart attack.

The neighbors were not happy about her death, so they called in the police. The doctor was arrested and there was a trial at which he confessed and explained how he deprived his wives of their lives. He tickled them. It appears that there are certain secret places on a woman's body, which, if she is tickled there, can make the woman laugh and go on laughing until it is too much for the heart and it bursts.

At that point Alik Beibutov, who had not been listening very carefully, poked Arshik in the back with his elbow.

Immediately opposite them Farida was sitting on the steps up to her veranda peeling potatoes with her legs wide apart. The folds of her short smock had slipped off her knees, revealing her fleshy white thighs disappearing into hidden depths.

Arshik and Alik exchanged glances. Without exchanging a word they started to pretend they were fighting. Rolling one over the other they landed almost at Farida's feet, where they kept playing around, taking it in turns to cast greedy glances where they could make out something black and hairy. Busy with her own thoughts, Farida did not at first pay any attention to the little boys scrambling around her feet. But then she realized what was going on, laughed and, still not bringing her legs together, said in a drawl: "Just look what a nosy little Armyashka we have here!"

For some reason or other she paid no attention to the equally nosy Alik Beibutov. For a long time Arshik continued to turn over Farida's words in his mind, but he could never figure out why he was called an "Armyashka" and not simply an "Armenian." It was particularly painful to him for another reason: that it was actually Farida who often appeared to him in his childhood dreams and provoked him with rounded knees and white thighs.

When he went to school Arshik realized that he was living among a quite different, foreign and not always very well-disposed people. "Armyashka!" they shouted at him on the very first day that Arshik entered the classroom.

Such insults were the main reason why Arshik had to get involved in fights practically every day—from the first day he attended school to the day he quit school altogether. He would come home one day with a black eye and another day with a swollen lip, and old Aramais would swear at him and tell him he was growing up to be a little thug. Arshik would say nothing, go off to school again the next day, and the same thing would be repeated: the open space overgrown with weeds, a crowd of boys around, and a fight. He was no longer afraid of pain. He was used to it. What depressed Arshik most was that his classmates never supported him with their shouts but cheered on his opponent, an Azerbaijani by nationality.

He quickly found the five-story building on Twenty-six Baku Commissars Street. There was a board in the entrance with a list of the occupants. Apartment eight, next to which was the name Oganyan, was underlined twice in chalk. Whistling cheerfully, Arshik dashed up to the fourth floor and pushed the bell at number eight.

Nobody replied. He waited a little and again pressed the bell. Still quiet as before. Arshik put his ear to the door and could hear quite clearly that there was somebody standing on the other side of it holding his breath. "Hey," he said quietly. "I have come from Mesropyan," he added, giving the name of Bella's father.

There was the clatter of a bolt, the door swung open and Arshik stepped back a little. He found himself face to face with a puny little man holding an axe at the ready. At the end of the corridor, holding a small child, was an equally insignificant little woman, pressed close to the wall.

"Hello!" Arshik said in Armenian. The man continued to hold the axe, ready to strike. "Mesropyan asked me to tell you that there's going to be a pogrom. You must hide."

"We have nowhere to go," the man said.

"Well, go to your relatives, your friends . . . " Arshik said hesitantly.

"Do you think things are any better for them at the moment?" the man asked with bitterness in his voice. Arshik didn't know what to reply to that. "Thank you, friend," the man slammed the door and the bolt slid home.

As he went down the stairway Arshik imagined to himself how those people would be sitting there alone in their flat for hour after hour, overcome by anxiety, trembling at every unusual noise, at footsteps on the street or the sound or a car stopping outside—and he shuddered.

He found nobody at all at home at the next address. But his insistent knocking caused a young woman in a nightgown to open the door of the next apartment and look out. "You want the Chinaryans?" she asked, looking Arshik over quickly.

"Yes. Where are they?" Arshik tried politely to keep his eyes off the woman's ample thighs.

"The Armyashkis have already bolted," the woman said, laughing.

"They could smell shashlyk in the air, and they've run away, the dogs!" Then she looked Arshik over again more attentively and decided, by scarcely detectable signs that are recognized only by people living in the Caucasus and Trans-Caucasus, that she was looking at another Armenian. "Akhmet!" the woman shouted joyfully. "Come here quickly— we've got another Armyashka here!"

A young man in his underwear burst out of the door and went straight for Arshik. But Arshik, who had taken part in so many street fights, skillfully dodged the blows aimed at him. Then Arshik managed to grab ahold of Akhmet's ears, and banged the head twice against his own knee. Blood spurted from Akhmet's damaged nose and with a look of wonder on his face, he sat down on the landing floor. The woman screamed and called the neighbors to help, but Arshik was already flying down the stairway.

The Mnyatsikanyani lived right in the center of the town. And on the same street, named after Lenin, was the last flat on Arshik's list, where the architect Kazaryan lived. The shortest way there was through the square. The closer Arshik got to it the more people there were on the streets, and the square itself was simply black with people. Some flakes of snow, rarely seen in those regions, were blowing around. In some places people had lit fires to keep warm. Men were gathered around them, passing bottles of wine, cracking jokes, and some of them even trying to dance. What the speakers on the square were saying could scarcely be heard, and nobody was listening to them very carefully.

Arshik zipped up his light windbreaker and boldly pushed his way into the crowd. He was still not really aware of the fact that he too was being hunted. That he was now a wolf. If anyone were suddenly to draw attention to the fact that he was an Armenian, those people standing around would tear him to pieces. Closer to the platform, the crowd was angrier and more aggressive. Speakers were shouting out: "Azer—bai—jan!"

"Ka—ra—bakh!"

"Clear the land of Armenians!"

They were waving green Islamic flags and singing patriotic songs. "The Soviet Government recognized back in the summer of 1920 that Nagorno Karabakh, Nakhichevan and even Zangezur should belong to Azerbaijan!" an intelligent-looking Azerbaijani with masses of gray hair shouted into a microphone. Arshik stayed to listen. "I will now read out loud what the President of the Azerbaijani Revolutionary Committee, Narimanov, wrote at that time to Lenin." The speaker reached into his pocket for some papers. "Here is the historic document!"

"They wanted to shit on the document!"

"Come on, get on with it!"

"Long live Azerbaijani Karabakh!" came a shout from the crowd and, instead of the intelligent Azerbaijani, a woman of uncertain age was pushed up on to the platform.

"My children . . . Fathers and sons . . ." she began haltingly. "I am a refugee from Nagorno-Karabakh." The crowd quieted down. One of the young men who had put the woman on to the platform pushed a microphone into her hand and whispered something into her ear.

"Where were you, I ask you," the woman continued, and her voice, now stronger, echoed around the whole square with a metallic sound. "Where were you when the Armenians dragged me, my little daughter and my old father by the hair out of our home and drove up onto the street? They took away all our possessions. They even took my engagement ring, the wicked devils." She held up her hand to show that there really was not an engagement ring on it. "Can real men, real Moslems allow the unbelievers to treat an Azerbaijani woman like that?"

The people around Arshik began to speak up, and there were some cries of indignation. Arshik listened to what was said along with the others and wondered, could what the woman was saying possibly be true?

"Shame on you!" cried the woman and burst into tears. The crowd broke into a roar and a part of it moved off down the main street. It was headed by a group of young people carrying metal bars, and they drew other people after them. Taking advantage of the confusion, Arshik avoided the square and turned into Lenin Street.

The houses he was looking for, numbers seventeen and nineteen, were not far from the corner. They were both three-story buildings, old and well built, with attractive stucco facades. As Arshik approached the first of them, he felt the crackle of broken glass beneath his feet. He looked up and saw that not only the glass but the frames, too, had been knocked out of all four windows. The walls around the windows were stained black from smoke. Arshik guessed that somebody had already been to the Mnatsikanyans', and had not only driven them out but had set fire to the place as well.

In number nineteen, the apartment he sought was on the first floor. It had also had its windows smashed, but there were curtains still hanging loosely in them. Arshik stood on tiptoes and looked into the flat. There were some people moving among the broken furniture. They were swearing at each other in Azerbaijani and gathering in bags those of architect Kazaryan's possessions that had survived. Arshik realized that there was nothing more he could do there.

Following the same route, but this time wisely avoiding the square, where the meeting was still going on, he went back to the market.

Bella was already waiting for him. Stamping her feet against the cold in her rather light shoes—a present from Arshik on her birthday—she was standing at the bus stop and looking from time to time rather nervously at her watch. "Are you frozen?" he called out.

Bella turned towards him, greatly relieved. "Arshik!"—and she immediately put her hand to her mouth. By calling out his name she was revealing to the people around that he was an Armenian.

"All in order," said Arshik quietly, because there were women standing next to them at the stop. So as not to upset Bella, he did not tell her anything about his visit to the last two addresses.

"I managed to warn them all!" Bella announced. "Now we'll go and pick up your father."

"The buses are not running downtown. Perhaps we had better go on foot?" But Bella had been rushing around all day, so they decided to wait for a bus or try to stop a taxi.

The women at the bus stop were loudly cursing the stall holders in the market. They had taken advantage of the absence of their Armenian competitors to raise the prices on everything. "It's the Armenians who keep stirring up trouble," one of them said.

A woman in a shabby coat looked curiously at Bella and Arshik. "She realized we're Armenian," Bella whispered.

"You and I are hiding ourselves as if we were smugglers," Arshik joked.

"It's even worse for us because we're Armenian. Only the police go after smugglers, but the whole town is after us," said Bella. "All right, let's go on foot."

At that moment the bus arrived at the stop. "Don't think of it!" said Arshik recklessly. "Your carriage awaits—let's go!"

Bella agreed, but suggested that, just in case, they should pretend not to know each other.

The bus was surprisingly empty, so there were enough seats for everyone who'd been waiting. Bella sat in front, while Arshik found a seat next to the woman in the shabby coat. The mustachioed driver headed off, first towards the part of Sumgait where Arshik lived.

It was evening. In the early twilight, out of the windows of the bus, could be seen first the depressing five-story tenements and then the rows of single-story private houses, with their shutters all tightly closed.

On Nizami street a group of young men and girls blocked the way for the bus. The driver honked at them, but they went on standing, forming a barrier right across the road. The bus came to a halt. The apparent leader of the group, a tough-looking man of about forty, approached the driver's door. "Why are you working?" he asked in strongly accented Russian.

"What?" The driver couldn't hear, so he dropped the side window.

"Why are you working, you bastard?" the man repeated angrily. "All honest people are on strike, and you're working."

"Got a family to feed," said the driver gloomily. "My children have to eat."

The whole group now gathered around the bus. "Maybe he's an Armyashka?" they suggested. "Take a good look at him, Muslim."

Excitedly and now in Azerbaijani, the driver swore by the health of his small son that he was a true Moslem, born in Agdam, and as proof he produced his driving license. Muslim studied the document carefully, compared the photograph with the driver's face, and then threw the license back at him. "He's an Azerbaijani," he drawled, disappointed.

The driver suffered the insults in silence. "Then he's a traitor to his own people," shouted one of the girls. A young man standing next to her brought his iron bar heavily down on the windshield of the bus and smashed it to bits. Muslim signaled to open the door. The driver, pale with fright, obeyed.

Muslim entered the bus and stood on the front platform. As he climbed in, his overcoat fell open to reveal a revolver stuck into his belt. With his legs wide apart, Muslim proceeded to study the faces of the silent passengers. He was in no hurry, obviously relishing his power over people. "Well," he said, "which of you has descended from Ararat to be with us in Sumgait?"

The passengers remained silent. The woman sitting next to Arshik took a sideways glance at him but also stayed silent.

Muslim passed between the rows of seats, staring into the faces first of one person, then of another, then stopped opposite Arshik. "Your mug seems familiar," he said thoughtfully. Arshik had also met Muslim in the market, in the company of some of the dealers. "You're an Azerbaijani, aren't you?"

"What else?" Arshik replied, looking him in the eyes. "Ask her." He indicated the woman in the tattered coat. "We live on the same block." The woman looked up, frightened, but nodded in confirmation.

Muslim went back to the front platform. He hadn't seen Bella, who was sitting behind his back. "It appears that all of you here are real Moslems." Muslim said in a tone of satisfaction. "These Armenian bastards are like cockroaches—they've hidden away in the cracks. But never mind, friends. We'll soon squeeze them out of Sumgait, and not only out of here—out of Nagorno-Karabakh as well. We'll get 'em even in Yerevan itself." Muslim was working himself up. "We'll declare Gazavat on them. We will write on the green banner of the Prophet: 'Death to the cowardly Armenians!'"

Bella stood up. "What do you want, kid?" asked Muslim, turning to look at her.

"I am an Armenian."

It was so unexpected that Muslim lost his head for a moment.

"I am an Armenian!" Bella repeated even louder.

Arshik was trembling inside himself, as usually happened before a fight. But, in a surprisingly quiet tone Muslim said merely: "Brave girl—I respect such people. Come along, I'll introduce you to my friends."

"There's no reason for me to get to know them," said Bella, her trembling voice giving her away.

"You scared?" Muslim smiled.

Bella hesitated for a moment and then, with a scornful shrug of her shoulder, she stepped out of the bus. Arshik was about to rush after her, but the woman in the shabby coat held him back. "Don't go!" she whispered. "They won't touch her, but they'll kill you!"

The crowd gathered around Bella and Muslim. Arshik could hear in the bus what Muslim was saying: "There you are, my friends. The girl is an Armyashka by nationality. She admitted it herself."

Somebody whistled in surprise. "What's your name?"

Bella didn't have time to answer before one of the girls intervened.

"Armenian slut—that's what she's called," the girl said contemptuously, and she spat in Bella's face.

Bella replied at once by giving her a good slap in the face. "I am an Armenian," she cried out. "Do you hear? Armenian!"

The passengers, including the stupefied Arshik, saw the girls rush on Bella and start scratching her face and tearing off her clothes. "An Armenian!" Bella cried out again, now quite hysterical.

Arshik rushed to help her, but the cowardly driver slammed the automatic door and began to reverse slowly away. "Open up!" Arshik begged him.

To the approving laughter of the men, the girls stripped Bella naked, leaving her only in her shoes. "Open up, you dog!" Arshik beat with his fist on the thick glass that divided the passengers from the driver's seat. "I'll kill you!" But the driver only increased speed.

Bella at last fought herself out of the clutches of the girls, who were howling with rage, and ran after the bus. She was followed by a group of laughing young men making indecent signs with their hands.

"Open up!" Arshik was now pleading. But the driver turned the huge bus around in one sweep and set off in the opposite direction. The white figure of the naked girl got smaller and smaller and soon disappeared around a bend. The bus raced down the street at a crazy speed, tossing the passengers from one side to the other. Now they too were screaming in panic, pleading for the bus to stop. Arshik sat alone, gripping the arms of his seat, with tears trickling down his face.

At an intersection the bus swerved sharply to avoid an oncoming truck, hit a lamp post and came to a stop. The driver leapt out of his seat and ran away, abandoning his bus to the mercy of fate. The passengers managed with difficulty to open the automatic doors and, one at a time, they scrambled out.

Arshik ran back the way they had come. He had lost his hat somewhere, and his hair was in a sweaty mess, stuck to his forehead. On the way he broke off a large stick from a fence and made up his mind that he was going to fight it out with those pigs, to the death.

But there was nobody there, not even the scattered bits of Bella's clothing. Arshik went everywhere on Nizami street, looking into the entrances to buildings and into the cellars, and in desperation he shouted out, calling out Bella's name. But the passersby backed away from him and quickened their pace.

The argument with Rustam touched old Aramais to the heart. Like all those who belong to small national groups, he knew and loved the history of his own people. Knowledge of that history gave him a feeling of his own dignity, a pride in belonging to a particular nationality. A member of one of the bigger nations, a Russian for example, had no need of such knowledge. His many fellow countrymen inspired him with self-confidence, and the national question was secondary. It wasn't so acute as it was for, say, the Georgians or the Jews.

It saddened Aramais to think that his neighbors the Azerbaijani had never heard about Gegart. Aramais reckoned that such a miracle of architecture should have been known to the whole world. The twelfth-century church of Gegart was situated only a few dozen miles from Yerevan. It was not the most ancient church in Armenia, but it was an amazing triumph of man's spirit and handicraft.

As you approach Gegart you first of all catch sight of a majestic cliff overgrown with wild bushes rising up to the blue sky. Stone steps, worn down through the years, lead to an almost invisible entrance. And once you have managed, bent double, to pass through it, you find yourself inside the church. The gigantic cliff is hollow inside. The church with its massive stone columns, stone altar, stairways, corridors and monks' cells has been carved out of the rock. The whole of the magnificent building is lit by diffused daylight pouring in from above, through openings cut in the top of the mountain.

Inside the church it is always quiet and deeply solemn. When Aramais first visited it with Susana, it seemed to him as though this holy place had been removed by Somebody from the hustle and bustle of everyday life and carefully covered by the palms of Somebody's hands. It was then they had learned how the church at Gegart had come to be built. Aramais was deeply moved by the story.

One day, early in the morning, eight hundred years ago, after having prayed to the east, a man clambered to the top of the cliff with the aid of a rope. There he took up a big hammer and a heavy chisel and started work. Day after day for forty long years, entirely on his own, this holy man hacked his way into the depths of the solid rock until he had fashioned within it the stone wonder that now rose before the astonished eyes of Aramais.

He believed that the church at Gegart was the Armenian people itself, infinitely laborious and talented. But when you reflect on its tragic history, steeped in blood and tears, you are inevitably reminded of the eastern saying: "When a stone falls on a jug, it's bad luck for the jug. And when a jug falls on a stone, it's bad luck for the jug again. It's always, always bad luck for the jug."

"Perhaps God turned his back on us?" Aramais thought to himself. "But why? What have we done to anger him, for him to condemn us to genocide, deprive millions of Armenians of their native land and scatter them around the whole world? It is said that the gypsies have been roaming from country to country for centuries without ever finding a place to settle because sometime or other they received a curse. It was gypsies who forged the nails by which Christ was nailed to the cross. But we Armenians—we built Gegart! That church is our character, our soul and our attitude to the whole of reality!"

Old Aramais glanced down the street. It was quiet, and there was no light showing in the windows of the house. That meant Arshik was not back yet. He went back to the table and sat down, resting his head in his hands.

When he was younger, Aramais had played an amusing game with himself. He had imagined a scene, as he took up his knife and thread—a huge government limousine with motorcycle escorts stops outside his shop, and out of it steps a man in expensive shoes, who makes straight for Aramais and says as follows: "Much respected Mister Aramais, we have had a long discussion at a meeting of the Politburo and we have come to a unanimous decision to appoint you First Secretary of Armenia."

"But why did you decide on me?" Aramais inquires, without letting them see how surprised he is. "After all, I'm not even a member of the Party."

"In this case it's of no importance. In the country of the Soviets everybody has equal rights, Communists and non-Party people alike. The main reason for our choice is that you are an honest working man. What is more, we are living in what is known as a people's state and we consider that there should be a working man at the head of each republic. And even your neighbors speak very well of you. We have made inquiries."

"I shall have to think it over," says old Aramais.

But the Chief Man of the Soviet Union is adamant. "There's no time for thinking things over—the international situation does not permit it.

Take up your duties now." And he hands Aramais a big red certificate framed in thin morocco leather. "It says here that you are the First Secretary. We are pinning our hopes on your good sense and love of your people." And with a ceremonial handshake for Aramais, the man gets into his limousine again and drives off, along with all his escorts.

Aramais scratches the back of his head in some confusion. But he doesn't remain in that state for long. He changes quickly into his best suit, leaves a note for Arshik explaining the situation, and sets off for the airport to take the first plane to Yerevan.

Outside the door of his house, three men in identical gray suits are waiting for him. "We are your personal bodyguards," they tell him.

"There is no need to protect me from my own people," old Aramais objects in a dignified tone. This does not please the bodyguards, but they obey—after all, they are dealing with the First Secretary of the whole Republic.

On arriving in Yerevan, Aramais does not go directly to his office in the Central Committee of the Party. He decides first of all to take a walk around the town, to look and to listen, to find out how the people are faring, what they are talking about, what they are worried about, and how the population is being supplied with goods.

There is a lot that doesn't please him. The shops are empty, the housing situation is even worse, and people are losing their tempers with each other at the slightest provocation. Children have become less fond of their parents and less respectful of their old folk. There are some dregs of society who have sunk so low that they steal the flowers placed in a graveyard so as to resell them. Aramais realizes that, by and large, with the Soviet regime now over seventy years old, the rust has begun to eat away at the souls of the Armenians. Thank God, at least they don't drink as much vodka as the Russians. They even take pride in the fact that unlike the other republics, not a single town in Armenia has to have a sobering-up center run by the police.

Finally old Aramais arrives in his office in the Central Committee. He immediately fires the fools and time-wasters and gets down to business. First of all he brings construction work on government offices to a complete halt and switches the workers thus liberated to the building of housing for people. He has all the churches in Armenia restored and opened to heal the spiritual wounds inflicted on the people. Then he arranges for the Catholicos of all Armenia to deliver a sermon every

Sunday on television. He puts through a special decree forbidding the bank to transfer any of the republic's resources into the military budget of the Soviet Union. In addition, young Armenians are no longer to perform their military service in the depths of Siberia, as has been the practice, but in their own native land. Armenia is roused, people find new life and happiness, and begin to work with real enthusiasm.

From Moscow there come repeated phone calls full of threats and demands that he withdraw his decrees, but Aramais pays no attention to any of this. But when he starts to abolish all the local Party committees and along with them the machinery of his own Central Committee, the alarming news is received that three tank divisions manned by Russian soldiers are advancing on Armenia from the Trans-Caucasus military region.

Even then old Aramais does not lose his head. He sets about creating a national army of self-defense, and takes part himself in building barricades on the streets of Yerevan and preparing fortified bases in the mountains from which to fight a guerrilla war. He appeals for help to all the Armenians living abroad and sends an appeal to the United Nations asking them to send their own armed forces. And when the Soviet tanks cross the Armenian border he is the first, with a gun in his hand, to mount the barricades.

Whenever he reached this point in the game old Aramais always came to a halt. His imagination could not tell him how the confrontation would end. He was inclined to realism in his thinking and he knew very well that Armenia had no chance against an angry bear like the whole Soviet Union. Then what would happen? Would he perish, or emigrate along with the whole people to Canada or Australia? Leave his homeland forever? And what about Gegart? And the graves with the remains of his ancestors? And Ararat?

He sought reassurance in the example of the Afghans. On the other hand, though Afghanistan was small, it was a separate country, whereas Armenia was a republic that had been a part of the USSR for seventy years. The Kremlin would not part with it so easily.

There was the sound of footsteps on the street, and voices, and old Aramais went out to see what was going on.

There was definitely something odd going on down there. At the end of the street there were some people moving about. Then they disappeared around the corner and their voices became fainter. "What a strange day," Aramais thought to himself, not for the first time, and he was about to turn back when a figure jumped out of a broken window in the ruined school. It pressed tightly against the wall, then staggered back and bumped into Aramais. It let out a cry and immediately turned a white face in his direction.

It was a girl of about fourteen, with two tightly plaited pony-tails, in a torn school uniform and an apron. "Who are you?" Aramais asked in Azerbaijani.

The girl continued to look at him in such horror that Aramais didn't know what to do. "What's happened to you, little girl?" he asked, this time in Armenian.

When she heard the sound of her own language the girl reached out as if to the light, put her arms around Aramais and, pressing herself to his chest, sobbed with a child's unconstrained despair. He let her have her cry and led her into the security office. "You just tell me everything and you'll feel better at once." Old Aramais put her on to the folding bed and covered up her legs with his padded jacket. "What is such a pretty girl called?"

"Anaid." The girl was still sobbing and sniffing.

Aramais immediately recalled another Anaid, Susana's mother, a good and wise woman. "Your parents gave you a beautiful name," said Aramais, taking our a handkerchief and making her blow her nose. "Now we'll have a drink of tea," he said, switching on the hotplate. "And I've found something sweet for you," and he took out of his pocket the candy that Lyoka had presented him with this morning, blew the bits of tobacco off it and placed it on the table

"You don't know what tasty tea I brew, do you? It's a real art if you know how." He went on talking, trying to divert the girl's thoughts from the shock that she had apparently just been through. "It was a Tadjik who taught me how to do it—we met a long way from here, in the Far North. First you pour the boiling water into the little teapot, do you see? Then you put in the tea and let it brew for five minutes."

The girl said quietly, "They were chasing after me out there, in the street." Then she added, "Please don't drive me out of here."

Pity for the girl brought a lump to Aramais's throat. He rolled a cigarette and said indistinctly, "Tell me about it."

On that day, as usual, Anaid had returned from school towards evening. Her parents were still at work. She had something to eat and sat at the table to do her homework. Then she heard the screech of a car braking sharply, and some shouting. She ran to the window and saw a big crowd of Azerbaijani boys. They blocked off the roadway and stopped a small car, from which they dragged a man, threw him down on the ground and started kicking him. At first the man uttered frightful cries, but later, when they took turns hitting him with iron bars, he made no more noise.

At that moment someone rang at the door of the apartment where Anaid lived. She was not inclined to open the door, but she thought it must be a school friend who had come—they had agreed to study together for an exam in trigonometry.

Anaid went to the door and called out: "Who's there?" In reply she heard the voice of old Ali-zade, a neighbor on the same floor and a very polite old man. Whenever he met Anaid in the courtyard, he always inquired how she was doing at school. On one occasion he had accompanied her father to a competition in gymnastics at which Anaid had gained second place among the schoolchildren of the district. That evening he had brought her a big box of chocolates, really delicious chocolates such as were not to be had in Sumgait. He had been sent them by a grandchild studying in Leningrad. Anaid opened the door and let the neighbor into the flat. Old Ali-zade immediately double-locked the door and told her she was not to show herself on the street because Azerbaijanis were killing Armenians.

"So that was what Hussein was warning me about," Aramais thought to himself. He asked the girl why she had not phoned immediately to her parents at work. "We don't have a telephone at home," Anaid said. "And old Ali-zade always seemed to be such a nice man."

"He started reaching up my skirt," she explained, blushing from shame. "But I am strong and I managed to break away!"

At that, Ali-zade had gone to the window and told her that if she didn't take off her school uniform herself, he'd call in the young men, who would rape her. Anaid did not look at Aramais as she spoke.

The girl had wept, and begged Ali-zade not do it. But the old man had already thrown open the window on to the street.

With the lecherous man looking greedily at her, Anaid started to unbutton her dress. But Ali-zade couldn't hold back and rushed again at the girl. In self-defense she grabbed her satchel full of text books from the table and hit him over the head. He fell down, and before he came to his senses she had managed to slip out the back door into the next street. The crowd, which had heard Ali-zade's cries urging them on, rushed after her. But she managed to trick them by hiding in the abandoned school.

The lid on the teapot was bobbing up and down and spitting out steam, but Aramais did not notice it. "My parents are probably back from work and looking for me," the girl said plaintively.

"If they're still alive," thought old Aramais. But aloud he told Anaid not to worry. "Tomorrow I'll take you home and explain everything to your mother and father."

"Why tomorrow—why not today?" The girl didn't understand. "My mother has a weak heart."

"Let those folk who were chasing you go back to their homes."

"All right," Anaid agreed obediently. "Only please lock the door, they might suddenly return."

"You have nothing to fear with me, Anaid," and Aramais pointed to his gun. "I have a weapon."

"Are they killing all the Armenians?" Anaid asked quietly.

Aramais looked into her eyes, still with a child's naive look in them, but in the depths of which could be seen the eternal suffering of her people, and he said with conviction: "No, my girl. You can't kill all the Armenians. There are not so many of us, but we are one of the most ancient peoples in the world. We have suffered invasions by many barbarians, who have burst into our home with swords flashing. Where are those people now? Even the most learned historians cannot remember what they were called. But we are still here. We are still living. And we shall continue to live. Because God has not filled our hearts with hatred and malice but with love for the world."

He made the girl drink some hot tea and put her again on the folding bed. Anaid suddenly giggled, recalling how Ali-zade's hands had trembled when she began to undo her dress. "What's the matter?" asked Aramais, rather alarmed. The girl was too embarrassed to answer, said nothing and closed her eyes. She was soon fast asleep. In sleep, her little face lost its anxious look, and her complexion returned to its rosy color.

Aramais could now think of nothing but Arshik. According to what the girl had said, something very strange was going on in the center of town. Knowing very well how his son's mind worked, he was afraid that he might get into big trouble.

EIGHT

Maksud told the taxi to stop a full block before he reached the address he was seeking. He ordered Khobot to wait for him in the taxi while he made his way on foot to the entrance of a quite undistinguished house. A couple of tough-looking men made way for him. They kept their hands pushed deep in the pockets of their raincoats.

"Gazavat," Maksud whispered the password.

"On the left and down the stairs," they told him.

"I know, brother." Maksud gave them a wink and went down into the semi-basement, where he found another man on guard.

Maksud gave him the password, and the guard pressed several times on the bell. The heavy door opened and Maksud entered "pogrom headquarters," the existence of which was known to few people in Sumgait. Here leaflets were printed and communications maintained. People like Maksud, leaders of the "hit groups," went there to receive their instructions, weapons, lists of Armenian addresses, and so on.

As he walked down the long corridor, past a number of closed doors, Maksud stopped at one of them and peered inside the room out of curiosity. He could hear a lot of groaning and crying from the people in the room. They were all "refugees"—drunks and drug addicts picked up off the streets—and they were rehearsing prepared stories about brutality by the Armenians against the Azerbaijanis in Nagorno-Karabakh. The next day they were due to go out onto the streets of Sumgait and provoke the crowds to resort to force.

If Maksud had been allowed into the room at the very end of the corridor, he would have come across the journalist who had particpated in the conference in Baku. Smoking one cigarette after another, his eyes were glued to the television screen. It was transmitting the evening edition of the nationwide current affairs program "Vremya." There were shots of a million-strong meeting in Yerevan and of workers on strike in Nagorno-Karabakh. Then, one after the other, the screen showed close-ups of people of various professions and trades, from other parts of the country. They were all expressing their "profound indignation" at the strike of solidarity organized by the people of Armenia and the people of Nagorno-Karabakh. The man from Baku had not exaggerated—the newspapers, radio and television of the Soviet Union were turning public opinion against the Armenians.

The telephone rang and the journalist grabbed the receiver. He was still hoping that the pogrom would be canceled and he would manage to extract himself from the whole business without having to get blood on his hands.

They were calling from Baku to inquire how things were going. The journalist assured them that everything was going according to plan. Then they asked him whether there were any correspondents from Moscow newspapers or—Allah preserve us—foreign publications in Sumgait. "Where could they come from?" the journalist asked, alarmed.

"In Nagorno-Karabakh this morning a patrol came across a wounded American reporter called Jacobson and took him by helicopter to the hospital in Baku. They took his films and tapes from him, but it is not impossible that one of his colleagues has got into the town secretly. Be on the alert."

The journalist promised he would, and then put down the receiver. He wiped the sweat from his forehead and for the hundredth time cursed himself for having gotten mixed up in such a dangerous adventure.

In another room, Maksud was being handed a packet of money, and the Makarov revolver he had long dreamed of owning. They made him sign for everything, and he then retraced his steps to the street and drove off in the taxi.

As old Aramais looked at the sleeping girl, he was reminded of that other Anaid, his late wife's mother. She had been a very thin, gray little woman, a teacher by profession, and she had survived by a miracle at the time of the Turkish massacre of 1915. She had been among those being deported to Deir-ez-Zor. Out of sixteen thousand people, only seven succeeded in escaping, with the help of a priest from the English mission.

Then the young Aramais had appeared in their home, to ask for the hand of the daughter Susana. He had been terribly lonely since the death of his father. Like all Armenians deprived of their native land, he was wandering around an alien nation like a pilgrim in search of a holy place, peace of mind and a sip of well water offered by kind hands.

"Woe betide the person who, if he falls, has no one to lift him up again," Susana's mother said then. "We all seek love and tenderness. So let this house become your house too. But you must take upon yourself our pain and our fate as well as your own."

She opened a photograph album. "There, look, that's my father on the first page." The photograph showed a man with a pointed beard and piercing eyes. "He was called Armenak." Anaid turned the page. "And that's my mother. She was called Zarik."

"Zarik," Aramais repeated, studying the faded features of young woman.

"That's Uncle Vachagan."

"Not so fast," Aramais said. He studied the photos as though he wanted to remember them all his life. "Which one did you say is Uncle Vachagan?"

"This one—in the fur hat."

"Is he still alive?"

"Vachagan was killed even before the deportation. They hung him by both legs upside down from a tree and hacked him to pieces with an axe. . . . And that's his wife Ardemis. That makes her your aunt. Look how young and beautiful she was. When the Turks started to drive us out of our homes, they raped her and then pinned her with big nails, still living, to the front door."

Aramais uttered a groan as if he were in pain and began to rock from side to side. "That is a photo of your elder sister Arpik," Anaid continued, in the same everyday tone of voice. "She perished when we had already been driven out of town and were on the open road. One of the soldiers, an elderly Turk with a long mustache, slit open her stomach and warmed his feet in it."

Aramais groaned. "It was before sunrise, and a very cold morning," Anaid explained. "And that's your father's younger brother, by the name of Ashot." She glanced at the photo with a tender smile. "When I was young I was very fond of Ashot and so was he of me. But for some reason or other he married my girlfriend, as usually happens. They sat Ashot in a chair and tied his legs. They then cut up his little three-year-old son on his knees. Then they stuffed bits of the boy's flesh into Ashot's mouth and made him eat it."*

Aramais let a long drawn out wail. "I can't! I just can't!" he shouted. "I just can't bear it!"

Susana also began to weep. "Mama, stop it."

"My heart is about to break," said Aramais in a whisper.

"You have to know the sort of burden you are taking upon yourself," Anaid said. "It really happened. It is the truth. I saw it all with my own eyes."

"I don't want to live any more," Aramais said.

"No, you must live. You have an obligation to carry on you own family line. You must have children."

"Why? So that they can live in this cruel world?" asked Aramais bitterly.

"And thank God for everything that exists, and rejoice at the beginning of every new day."

"After all that, you can go on believing in God?"

"In God within man, making him magnanimous and reasonable."

"God in man? But man is a beast! Only instead of an animal skin he wears a suit made by a tailor!"

"Nevertheless I continue to believe it," Anaid said firmly.

"Then tell me where God was in them when their hands were committing such crimes!"

"Those people's minds were disturbed."

"They lived their lives and were normal people and all of a sudden their minds were disturbed? How did that happen? What sort of nasty bug had bitten them?"

Anaid closed the album and placed it on her lap. "I believe it happened like this," she said. "One day someone whispered to a neighbor:

* All the incidents cited are fully documented.

'It seems to me that those people living across the street do not cross themselves with the correct hand.' The neighbor agreed, although it was all the same to him who made the sign of the cross with which hand. But the neighbor didn't like the fact, for example, that the people across the street had a bigger house than his. He was too lazy to build one like theirs, or maybe he hadn't enough money. But it offended him to see every day that someone was living better than he. What he said, however, was: 'They are of a different religion. And, just look, neighbor, their noses are not like ours.'"

Aramais could not agree at the time that such madness as the genocide of 1915 could flare up just because of some trifling matter of religion or personal envy. "It's just impossible to believe," he said.

"But why?" Anaid objected. "A big river also begins as a little stream. What's more, those people didn't know what they were doing. I'm sorry for them."

"After all you've seen, you can be sorry for them?" Aramais couldn't believe his ears.

"I don't forgive them. But I also weep for them."

"How have they earned your tears? Tell me, I'm too stupid to understand."

"The people whose hands committed such a terrible deed, even if afterwards they lived long lives . . . " Anaid was trying to explain to him what she had come to believe as she turned it over in her mind through long sleepless nights. "Those people can never again be happy or know peace of mind. Not on a sunny spring morning, nor in love for a woman, nor in the birth of a child. However deeply they try to hide the truth, their memories will always retain the sight of Ardemis crucified on the door, and of Vachagan hacked in two, and of the unfortunate Ashot with the child on his tied knees. The horror of what they did will be passed on to their children, their grandchildren and their great-grandchildren. In killing us, they killed themselves."

The woman who spoke had herself lived through the whole horror of the massacre, and then had come to this surprising conclusion: the man who strikes down another is primarily killing himself.

Late in the evening of February 26, General Kramarenko received from Simonov a detailed account of what was happening in Sumgait, and he realized that the time had come to act. He knew that after the morning meeting of the Politburo the General Secretary had left Moscow, to spend Saturday and Sunday in the Crimea, at his favorite holiday home on the Black Sea.

Kramarenko called for an official car and set off for the military airport near Moscow, where a plane belonging to the KGB awaited him. The general had decided against phoning the Gensec's assistants and asking for permission to meet with him. First because among the people around the head of state there was certainly one of the Big Man's informers, and, second, because they might arrange for Kramarenko to be received on the Monday, February 29, when the events in Sumgait would be irreversible.

Three hours later, the plane landed at Simferopol. The navigator opened the door of plane and put out some metal steps. Kramarenko caught the real scent of spring. After Moscow, with its freezing cold and snowstorms, it was strange to see the green tips of the trees, the palms with their rustling leaves, and the almond blossoms.

The Gensec kept Kramarenko waiting a long time in his living room—a big room with tall, diamond-shaped windows looking out on the sea. A naval vessel could be seen out there, preserving the General Secretary's peace and quiet.

As he waited for the Secretary to see him, Kramarenko reflected on the different ways fate had dealt with the two of them. Years ago, as an officer in the secret police, he had recruited a young communist activist into his service in a little town far from Moscow. Now Kramarenko had still not reached retiring age, but that young man could oblige him, a lieutenant-general, to wait patiently for an audience. The young man was now in a position to decide the fate of not just individual people, but whole nations. How and why the choice of a successor to the already terminally sick Andropov fell on this young man nobody knew. He had a certain charm as a person, he spoke quite well, and he had a university education. But it was more likely to have been a matter of chance, like Korolev's choice of Gagarin, who had been just one of a whole team of cosmonauts.

The Gensec had a look of annoyance on his face when he came in— he didn't like being disturbed in his holiday house, especially without a preliminary phone call. He didn't offer to shake hands, and simply nodded stiffly at the general who rose to greet him. But when Kramarenko had recounted the ominous events taking place in Sumgait, and the role that the Big Man was playing in that dirty business, and then produced the evidence, the Gensec changed his manner altogether. He realized what a powerful weapon against his rival the general was placing in his hands. If these documents could be exploited intelligently, it would be possible to squeeze the Big Man into a corner, and his supporters in the Central Committee would keep their tails down.

"Wait a moment, general, I'll be back right away." The Gensec stood up and went quickly across to a special communications room equipped with lots of telephones. He called the commanding officer of the parachute troops and, without going into details, ordered him immediately to transfer a military unit to Sumgait by air.

The Gensec was now so well-disposed towards Kramarenko that he even suggested they should visit together the old wine cellars in Massandra. Accompanied by two security cars, the enormous bullet-proof ZIS-111 limousine floated out of the gates and sped along the twisting Crimean road. Far ahead of them raced a police car, with its lights flashing and a loudspeaker ordering all oncoming cars to get into the side of the road. At all the intersections and side roads, officers of the highway police were on duty controlling the traffic.

"Why have you and not Granddad come to report to me about the events yesterday in Sumgait?" the Gensec asked suddenly, calling the Chairman of the KGB by the nickname his colleagues used. The general remained diplomatically silent. "I realize that KGB men don't criticize the boss, but they do like to talk about him," remarked the Gensec subtly, and looked expectantly at the General.

Kramarenko understood what the Gensec wanted to hear from him, so he replied cautiously, without spelling everything out. "Granddad is tired. One must not forget that he is advanced in years. I have the impression that, if he were to be offered a prominent position, but one that was not too burdensome, he would grasp it with both hands."

The Gensec guessed what lay behind those words. Granddad would then become his loyal supporter, if he were given a sinecure position that left him with the right to use, as before, all the good things provided by the Kremlin—a country house, special shops closed to the public, and the Kremlin hospital, which was by no means unimportant at his age.

They said no more about official business until the cortege of cars drew up at the famous Massandra wine cellars. Having been previously warned, the management of the cellars had laid new asphalt in the entrance gateway, cleaned out the whole area, slapped on some white-wash and put some paint on the old building where possible—and where it wasn't, they had covered things up with huge red banners calling on the people to carry out Party decisions.

In the courtyard, standing in a line, they found the director, the secretary of the Party organization, the chairman of the factory committee, the secretary of the Young Communists' Organization and three representatives of the working class—all in blindingly white smocks.

The General Secretary and Kramarenko got out of the limousine and cast their eyes over all the magnificence. "Prince Potemkin and his 'sham' village," the Gensec commented generously, "are lodged deep in the memory of our officials."

They were taken on a long tour of the underground cellars, with their gigantic barrels. The director talked intelligently and interestingly about ways of producing wine, explained the subtleties of wine-tasting, and presented the visitors with some vintage wines from a special reserve.

The General Secretary was obviously very pleased with the excursion. The director noticed this, and when the General Secretary was signing his name in the book for distinguished guests, he suddenly began to describe to him a wine-growing tragedy. It appeared that, in order to be ahead of the whole country in the campaign against alcoholism, the local Party authorities had given orders for all the vineyards in the Crimea to be cut down. Thousands of acres of vines had already fallen under the bulldozer. The chief wine-grower in the region, a doctor of science, tired of fighting with them, had committed suicide.

"Make a fool pray to God and he'll crack his head open!" exclaimed the Gensec crossly, and he instructed his assistant to get in touch with the local authorities the next day and tell them to stop doing such outrageous things.

"Yes," the General agreed, "if they go on campaigning like that it won't be long before we have to import grapes from Spain. For hard currency."

"Just imagine," the Gensec went on indignantly. "These stupid folk keep on taking the result for the cause! Yes, there is a government decree on the campaign against drunkenness and alcoholism. Then let's not produce any wine but harvest the grapes and send them to the northern parts of the country, where there is such a need of vitamins.

But they chop them down! You can do anything for these people, and it does no good at all." He waved his hand helplessly, upset by the eternal sloppiness of the Russians.

The General Secretary was silent all the way back to the house, his face knit in a frown. The General, sitting next to him, also said nothing. Back there in Massandra he had had a very interesting idea, connected with Sumgait. It was a dangerous idea, but if it came off the general could win a game in which the stakes would be the post of Chairman of the KGB. "Why worry about the danger?" he said to himself. "The man who doesn't take a chance doesn't drink champagne, but swills down plonk from the Massandra cellars."

His idea, to which the Gensec listened with great attention, was this: it was one thing for the events in Sumgait to be brought to a halt by the government before they got under way. In that case, the Big Man would still have the possibility of extricating himself from a difficult situation. But if it flared up into a real pogrom, and there was bloodshed, that would no longer be just information provided by some driver or journalist from Baku. It would be a tragic reality that would evoke a widespread reaction both in the Politburo and among the mass of the people. It would attract attention even abroad. And that would surely mean the end of the Big Man. He would lose his disproportionate influence in the Party, and it would then be possible to remove him quietly from the political scene. As for the immediate matter of Sumgait itself, in two or three days' time they could transfer a military unit there and bring the disorder there to a brutal end. That would, incidentally, show all the discontented Tatars, Baltic and other peoples that the Soviet regime was still ruling with a firm hand.

And it would be a good lesson for the too independent-minded Armenians. They would soon realize that they could not survive surrounded by Moslems without their Russian big brother. In short, they ought to let events in Sumgait go their own way. "In this way we will kill two birds with one stone—we will bring the Big Man down and at the same time bring some order into the national question in the country. Of course, I shall keep my finger on the pulse of Sumgait all the time," the General said in conclusion. The General Secretary and the KGB General thought in identical terms.

The Gensec looked out over the sparkling sea and kept his silence. It was only as the limousine drove into the courtyard of the house that he turned to Kramarenko and said, "I'm glad that the Committee for State Security has people who are both energetic and able to think in modern terms. People like you, Semyon Vasilevich."

It was the first time in years that the Gensec had called the General by his first name. The General realized he had won the game.

The planes were already in the air and heading for Azerbaijan when the officer in command of the parachute detachment received a message by radio from his commanding officer to cancel his earlier orders. The huge ANTE transport planes performed a sweeping turn and headed back to the airport near Moscow where they were permanently based.

Meanwhile, the center of Sumgait was already seething with real revolt. The police simply watched passively as half-drunk noisy crowds of people staggered down the streets. The windows of shops and houses were being smashed by young people. Cars burned on the street. And dozens of Armenians had been injured, tortured and killed in their own homes.

Thoroughly shaken by what he had seen, Arshik was ready to go to work with his knife himself. But his most important task now was to warn his father, and to hide him somewhere before the wave of carnage reached their part of town. So he ran off to find his father by the shortest route—without even thinking that in the more populous places he could be recognized and exposed by his Azerbaijani acquaintances.

On the way, Arshik decided to slip into his home to get money and some papers. He turned onto his street, but immediately stepped back to hide behind the corner. He had seen Khobot and Maksud chasing after some girl in a school uniform. Arshik saw them lose sight of her in the darkness and go off, cursing their luck. He also saw his father take the girl into his workplace. So he waited until all was quiet, then crept cautiously into his own home. Without putting a light on, he gathered up all he needed and locked the door behind him.

But Arshik had not taken account of the fact that he was dealing with a cunning and very experienced thief. Maksud had pretended to be going off with Khobot to the center of town, but in fact he had turned back by a roundabout route and had set up an ambush next to the workshop. He intended to take advantage of the situation to settle accounts with old Aramais, and at the same time to catch the girl and rape her.

They caught Arshik by the workshop. Khobot grabbed him by the hair and dragged him through the ruins and into the room where Arshik had played with the other boys so often as a child. "Maksud," Khobot called out. "I've caught the stupid little Armyashka."

Maksud, still in his long coat and fur hat, strode into sight in the circle of yellow light thrown by a street lamp. "So we meet again, Arshik," he said with excessive friendliness.

"You'll get your boots tomorrow, Maksud, I swear it!" Arshik protested. "On the holy cross, Maksud!"

Maksud shook his head reproachfully and, turning to Khobot, said, "He's still out to deceive poor Maksud." Khobot tugged at Arshik's hair and banged his head against the wall.

"I've had a lot of work, Maksud, I just didn't have the time!" Arshik still hoped to get away with his life.

"How much time do you need, huh? You got an advance from me back in the summer."

"Everyone does that!"

"You promised to make me a pair of boots. Of kid, with white welts. Squeak, squeak!" Maksud said, imitating Arshik.

"Tomorrow, Maksud!" Arshik pleaded. "Or if you want I'll run home now and bring you the money!" It was a rather feeble attempt to trick Maksud.

"Now just think back, Arshik," Maksud continued, still with the same smile on his face. "How many times have I been to the workshop and you have avoided me?" He again turned to Khobot "Tell me, is that really the way to behave?" Instead of a reply, Khobot again banged Arshik against the wall. "Do you admit you're to blame?"

Colored stars danced before Arshik's eyes. "Don't hit me, Maksud," he begged in a quiet voice. "I'll work all night to have the boots ready for you tomorrow."

"Let him go," Maksud ordered Khobot.

Arshik stood unsteadily between them, his arms hanging down helplessly at his side. "As for the boots, all right, you'll let me have them tomorrow," Maksud agreed graciously. "And now tell me where the girl in the school uniform has hidden herself?"

"I don't know any girl," Arshik said. "Haven't seen one."

"He's out to deceive me again, Khobot," said Maksud, offended. "I forgive him everything and he doesn't like me."

To himself, Arshik thought, "So that was why, on Nizami street, she didn't call out to me by name or call for help—so as not to give me away," realizing it for the first time.

"Shall I put the knife in?" suggested Khobot.

Arshik suddenly butted him in the stomach with his head and tried to break out into the street, but Maksud managed to trip him up and he fell to the ground. Khobot gave a roar and kicked Arshik several times with all his might. "Don't kick a man when he's down," Maksud said. Khobot stopped.

Arshik hesitated a little, then got to his feet.

"Tell me where the girl is hiding and I'll let you go."

"I don't know." Arshik covered his face with his arm.

"Hit him, Khobot."

There was a dull thud. Something in Arshik cracked and he slid down the wall to the ground. "Get up, Arshik," said Maksud. "Go on, I said get up!"

Arshik got up onto his hands and feet, shook his head, and with difficulty stood up. His face was all swollen and looked more like a mask than skin. "Father!" he wanted to call out, knowing that old Aramais was not far away. "Father!" But all that came from his throat was a faint wheezing sound.

"There's nothing I can do for you, my dear Arshik," Maksud said regretfully. "It turns out that the wise folk were right when they said to me: 'Maksud, only the grave will straighten out an Armenian.'" With a sudden quick movement he shot his hand forward, holding a long, razor-sharp knife. Arshik gave a strange gulp and collapsed at Khobot's feet.

"The girl is hiding with his old man in the warehouse," Maksud said confidently as he put the knife away. "That's why he wouldn't talk."

"So let's call on the old man," Khobot agreed as he searched the pockets of the dead Arshik. "And look, there's money here." He whistled in surprise at finding the whole bundle of money that Arshik had saved up for his father. "Look, Maksud, how much the Armyashka had put together!"

"He was an honest boy, Arshik was." Maksud divided up the money and handed some to his friend. "He knew he would meet up with me today and wanted to repay his debt. For the Polar boots with the white welts."

The key in the door of the security room turned quietly on its own. There was a click as the lock opened. Old Aramais was dozing, but he immediately opened his eyes, a habit of many long years in prison camps—to be always on the alert, even when asleep. "Somebody with a lock-pick has turned the key from the other side," Aramais guessed, but continued to sit still in his place.

The door began to open, but was stopped by the safety chain. Then a hand with very delicate white fingers came through and began to feel around, seeking to release the chain. Aramais put his hand on the teapot and found it was still hot. Treading softly he went to the door and poured the boiling water over the intruder's hand.

There were loud curses on the other side of the door, and then somebody threw himself with all his force against it.

Anaid woke and sat up in fear and trembling on the bed. Aramais put his finger to his lips to warn her not to make a sound. Somebody hit the door again with his shoulder. "I shall shoot," Aramais said and noisily clicked the bolt on his rifle. There was the sound of another mighty blow at the door. The chain would not hold out long with such treatment.

Aramais fired into the gap between the door frame and the door. Outside someone let out a scream and jumped aside. Aramais quickly slammed the metal-framed door shut, and locked it again with the key.

There followed a lengthy period of silence. Aramais began to think the raiders had gone away, but then he heard the insinuating voice of Maksud. "Aramais—we don't want you. Give us the girl. Her mother is looking for her."

"It's not true, it's not true," Anaid whispered. "Don't believe them, please."

Aramais again put his finger to his lips. Trying not to make a noise, he moved the table over to a ventilation opening in the wall and with difficulty managed to get himself up to it. Then he signalled to the girl to hand him his rifle. Now he could see who his visitors were.

Right by the door, with his ear pressed to it, stood Maksud, and further away, under a lamp, his strong-man friend Khobot was bandaging up his leg, which had been hit by the bullet.

Maksud scraped on the iron door with the long nail of his little finger. "Dear Aramais," he called out. "Your little pop gun won't help. Anyway why do you have to offend poor Maksud? You know very well that I can catch your Arshik and put the knife to him. So let's not quarrel."

Aramais looked at his house behind the workshop and saw that, as before, there were no lights in the windows. "So long as Arshik doesn't come back now," Aramais prayed to God, never suspecting that his murdered son was lying quite close.

"And nothing will happen to the girl. She'll simply get to know a couple of years sooner what it is to have a real man."

Anaid was seized by a nervous trembling. "I'm waiting for your answer, Aramais." Maksud pulled his revolver out of his belt and slipped off the safety catch. "Take pity on your son, old man. He's so young and so bright. The boy needs to live so you can look after his children later."

Suddenly, with his thief's animal instinct, Maksud sensed that Aramais was watching him, and he fired three times at the ventilator opening, without aiming, at random.

Aramais recoiled from the opening and only just managed to stay on the table. The bullets sent brick dust all over him. "Lie down on the ground, Anaid," Aramais said, fearing that a bullet might ricochet and hit her.

Anaid lay down immediately and pleaded: "Only don't hand me over, Aramais, I beg you."

"Don't let the thought enter your mind, my dear." He loaded his rifle again. He had only two bullets left in his pocket. He remembered that he had a whole unopened pack at home and clicked his tongue in regret. How could you tell when they would be needed? He had watched over the warehouse for so many years and had never once had to use a weapon.

Meanwhile Maksud had run across to his friend and started explaining something to him vigorously, pointing first at the warehouse, then towards the town center.

A boyish figure appeared at the end of the street. "Arshik!" Aramais thought, in cold fear.

Maksud and Khobot noticed the boy as well and beckoned him towards them. "Run for it!" Aramais shouted desperately through the opening. "Run back, son!"

But the boy only quickened his steps and then ran into the workshop where the thieves were waiting for him.

Aramais pushed the barrel of the rifle into the vent, quickly wiped the sweat from his face, took aim and fired. Maksud clutched his head with his hands and fell to the ground. Khobot stayed frozen to his place in amazement. Aramais pushed the last bullet into the rifle and fired again, this time at Khobot.

There was the sound of breaking glass in the workshop. The young man who looked like Arshik stood still.

"Missed him," Aramais said regretfully, noting that he would have to call in a repairman the next day.

With unexpected speed for such a big man, Khobot ran off limping down the street, followed by the other boy. "So it wasn't Arshik," said Aramais, greatly relieved. He jumped off the table and opened the door. "Run for it!" he said to the girl. "Get away while there's no one there!"

Anaid huddled into a corner.

"What's the matter with you, now?"

"I'm afraid!" the girl looked like a little animal driven into a corner. "Only along with you, Aramais!"

"I can't," he said, trying to persuade her. "I must wait for my son here."

"No!"

"Who do you think you're talking to?" Aramais shouted at her. "They'll be back any moment."

He dragged the resisting girl out of the office. "Run over there to the bus stop, get into a bus and get away somewhere as far as possible from here. Don't go home—better spend the night with a school friend, an Armenian."

"Don't chase me out!" Anaid clung on to him for dear life, and old Aramais gave in. He realized that she was so scared that she was probably unable to think clearly, and could easily get into real trouble again. Nobody knew what exactly was going on in the town.

"Stay here," Aramais said, "I'll be right back."

He crossed the road and bent over Maksud. There was very little blood—the bullet had hit him in the temple. "So you've earned yourself five years, you old fool," Aramais muttered out loud. "Exceeding the demands of justified self-defense" was how the article in the Criminal Code was phrased.

He picked up Maksud's revolver and returned to the warehouse, where Anaid was standing nervously in the doorway. "Is he dead?" she asked in a little voice that trembled.

Aramais said nothing. He removed the cartridge clip from the revolver to reveal four greased yellow bullets sticking out. "You killed him?" Anaid looked at Aramais with amazement in her eyes. "Because of me, was it?"

"For your sake, for my sake and for the sake of others." Aramais pushed the girl back into the security office and locked the door. "Take the mattress off the bed, put it in that corner and sit on it." He pointed to the safest place for her, while he clambered up on the table again to wait for Arshik.

As before, there was nobody on the street, but the dark outlines of people glued to their window panes could be seen in the neighboring houses.

"Yes, five years of general service in a labour camp," Aramais thought to himself as he looked at the dead body lying near the workshop. "The court ought to take into consideration my age and also the fact that I'm a war veteran. But what will happen to Arshik now? He'll get into bad company and become the same sort of bandit as that damned Maksud." And he heaved a heavy sigh.

Just then a couple appeared, walking down the dimly lit street. A very smartly dressed young man, obviously an Azerbaijani, had his beau, equally well turned out, by the arm. They were apparently about to spend the evening in the only cinema in the district, or perhaps they had been invited out somewhere.

Outside the workshop the woman stepped on the spread-eagled body and let out a scream. The man bent over Maksud and then said something to her and calmly continued on their way, taking him for a sleeping drunk.

"Good Lord, what a day to have sent us!" Aramais drew his hand across his face. "But were there ever good days?" The Turkish massacre, an impoverished and hungry childhood, the restless wandering about after the death of his father, the war, the postwar devastation, the prison camp, and this dreary life going on day after day and year after year. "No!"—he suddenly remembered. There had been such a joyous hour and day in his life. It was a day that Aramais remembered down to the smallest detail—every word that had been spoken then, every smile, every glance. He had preserved it in his heart like a fledgling bird and had never told anybody about it, not even Arshik. Memories like that must be kept just for oneself—they act as a life preserver to keep a person from going right to the bottom.

It happened in the summer at the end of the thirties, in a little town on the Black Sea coast of Bulgaria. In his mind's eye Aramais could see again the little courtyard with a vine trailing over it, a well, a veranda and a house—a modest dwelling for two women.

There was nobody in the courtyard, which was dotted with rays of sunlight. And it was quiet, except for the sound of music coming from some neighbors. To the accompaniment of an Armenian instrument, two voices, a man's and a woman's, were repeating the words of a sad Armenian melody:

> *Exiles, the pitiful amputated fragment*
> *Of a people who have suffered every torment.*
> *In a strange land far from home*
> *Pale and hungry they huddle in their huts*
> *And drink and drink . . .*

The singers were only just learning the song, because they would repeat some of the couplets in a different key, and sometimes they would simply remain silent as the musician tuned his instrument.

Old Aramais could see himself as he was then—young and strong, in his straw hat and a chequered "American" shirt, very fashionable at the time. He stood at the gate and looked in silence at the house, but could not make up his mind whether to enter. It was where his father had died, but it was now occupied by strangers. But then the two voices began to sing the heart-rending song:

> *Their native land is now a desert,*
> *Their family home burnt down and wrecked;*
> *Refugees, they wander in foreign parts . . .*

With that, Aramais pulled himself together and went into the courtyard. "Father," he said quietly. "I've come back, father." Aramais knelt down and kissed the worn steps of the porch. "I'm back."

> *And they sing, and their wild songs pour forth*
> *As though their hearts were breaking.*
> *Rage overcomes them, they've no air and no space*
> *And their tears flow and flow without end.*

It was then that Susana appeared. She was wearing a light flowered dress and carrying a handbag. "Hey!" she cried out to Aramais from the gate. "What are you doing, sir?"

Aramais stood up, rather embarrassed. "I tripped over—"

"You haven't hurt yourself?" Her dark eyes expressed genuine concern "Can I help you?"

"Did I hurt myself?" Aramais repeated her words. "I suppose you could say so," he hinted. In those days he often wept all night out of loneliness.

But the girl took his words at face value and demanded that he show her his leg. "It's not my leg that hurts," Aramais confessed.

Susana understood. "Hey!" she said with a kindly smile. "Life goes on! The sun still shines and the vine still blooms!"

Aramais studied the girl attentively and realized that it was not just belonging to the same nationality or bearing the same family name that brought people together. A person quite unknown to you, whom you meet by chance along the road, can become your brother, so long as he hears the same song that is sounding within you. And you, in turn, can understand that the same melody is coming from his breast, too.

That day, two people met, and sang in harmony.

The sound of a motorcycle approaching was heard. The light of the headlight was reflected in the windows of a house and the motorcyclist burst into the street. But it was not a traffic policeman. Khobot was sitting in the sidecar.

The motorcycle came to a halt outside the workshop. The rider left the motor running and along with Khobot lifted Maksud's body off the ground and into the sidecar. With a frightened glance at the door of the warehouse, Khobot climbed up behind the rider. The machine turned sharply, and they zoomed off, back to the town center.

Old Aramais was watching his house. Arshik had still not put in an appearance. There was no light in the windows. The girl, asleep on the mattress, exclaimed in her sleep and turned on to her other side.

Old Aramais half-closed his eyes and could again see, with all the precision of a photograph, another house—the one there in Bulgaria. He was lying on the divan, on which his father had died, and he could see the sun's first rays shining through the closed shutters. "Bam-m . . .

Bam-m . . . Bam-m . . . " the clock on the town square rang out the hours. And immediately afterwards the church bells rang out with a different tune: "Tilini-bom, tilini-bom, bom!" calling the faithful to matins. Then again all was silence except for the sound of cautious footsteps on the squeaky floor. It was Anaid, Susana's mother, who had already risen and was going to the kitchen to light the stove.

"Mama!" Susana's sleepy voice came from the next room. "Where's my dressing gown?"

And her mother muttered in reply: "Quiet, my dear, you'll wake Aramais. Let him sleep."

"Let him sleep, let him sleep!" Susana began to sing and her vague outline could just be made out behind the curtain. They believed Aramais was asleep, but in fact he was lying there listening to the amazing world outside the walls of the house. He was absorbing the birdsong in the courtyard, the voices of neighbors calling to each other, the crunch of a cart on the street, the belated crowing of the rooster, announcing the beginning of another day.

Aramais was again on his guard: the sound of motorcycles again, followed by a vague hum of human voices and the noise of many tramping feet. From around the corner emerged a great crowd of Azerbaijanis. They were carrying the body of Maksud, the man he had killed, the head hanging helplessly back. Little boys were running ahead of the crowd and several motorcyclists were circling around, the visors on their helmets pulled down.

The crowd approached the warehouse. "This is where he is!" said Khobot, jumping out of the sidecar. "This is where the bastard is hiding!"

"Death to the Armyashki!" came a shout from the crowd.

A few of the young people ran across to the warehouse and began to bang on the door with iron bars. Old Aramais put his hand out of the ventilation hole and fired a warning shot. The young people backed away and the whole crowd retreated to the other side of the street. The girl was wakened by the sound of the shot. "Lie down, Anaid," Aramais said. "And cover your ears with your hands."

The girl lay down again and obediently pressed the palms of her hands to her ears, revealing her ink-stained fingers.

Attracted by the noise, Aramais's neighbors began to come out of their houses. He saw Stepa, Aida and Farida, and he even caught sight of Rustam's scarred features. The crowd kept growing. All the people kept shouting, not listening to each other, gesticulating furiously, pointing at Maksud's body, which was still being held high like a banner, and then at the warehouse where Aramais and the girl were taking refuge.

Khobot smashed the window of the shoemaker's shop, seized a torch from a small boy and began to set the shop alight. Lyoka, the poor idiot boy, kept rushing from one neighbor to another, appealing for help, and then tried to put the fire out. Khobot struck him with his powerful fist and brought him to the ground. One of the motorcyclists sprinkled some gas on the fire from a small can, and the workshop was quickly engulfed in a real blaze. Old Zeinab came rushing out of her house with a bucket of water, but the other women, led by Farida, grabbed her, tipped the bucket over and pushed her back into the yard.

"Nothing to be sorry about," Aramais consoled himself as he watched the fire consume the workshop where he had spent so many years bent over other people's footwear. "It is now certain that if the police do not turn up, the fire brigade surely will. With them around, the crowd will be afraid to take the law into their own hands."

Time passed, but neither the police nor the fire trucks put in an appearance. The young men on their motorcycles continued to weave about, making a deafening noise with their engines, and the crowd became steadily more excited. The people, their faces illuminated by the fire at the workshop, were already working themselves into a frenzy. Aramais saw that even his neighbors had the same wild look on their faces and the same raging hatred in their eyes. The very same people with whom he had lived for so many years in the same building and who that same day had been sitting together with him at the same funeral table drinking wine—those people were now, like all the others, working themselves up into a fury opposite the warehouse, waving their fists and shouting filthy, insulting curses.

"What harm have I done to them?" Aramais said to himself bitterly as he watched his neighbors. "Have I ever struck one of them, deceived them or said an unkind word about anybody? Is it because we pray to different gods? But that's the way it always was. The Soviet regime has turned everyone away from religion, and now no one believes in anything. Maybe it's life itself that has made them so bitter? But the Armenians don't live any better than they do. Does that mean it's not to do with religion or nationality, but with man himself? Simply that, for most of the time, the animal side of him is hidden within him, but when this sort of day comes along he throws off his human mask and bares his fangs?"

"In killing us they kill themselves." Aramais recalled Anaid's words. "These people will never be able to be really happy or find peace within themselves. Not on a sunny spring morning, nor in love for a woman, nor at the birth of a child."

Now that they knew that Aramais was armed, the crowd was still afraid to move close to the warehouse. Some of the little boys became more daring, however, and wanted to demonstrate their courage to their elders, so they would run up to the door, spit at it and shout, "Stinking Armyashka!"

Suddenly, old Aramais caught the smell of burning rubber. The thugs had managed to set fire to the store. They had discovered in the rear wall yet another air vent, sprayed some gas through the hole and thrown in a burning rag. The security office started to fill with the pungent smoke. The girl couldn't stop coughing. Their eyes began to fill with tears. "Not long before we'll *have* to go outside," muttered old Aramais, although he knew full well that it would be the beginning of the end—the crowd would tear him and Anaid to pieces.

He came down from the table, soaked his padded jacket with water from the tap and lay down on the ground, covering himself and the girl with it. That made it easier to breathe. "All the same, we can't hold out for long. We will be either suffocated or burned to death."

"What did you say, Aramais?" Anaid asked, half-choking. She was again seized by a nervous trembling.

"I was saying, my dear child," Aramais said hoarsely into the girl's ear, "that I am now going to get up and go outside."

"And I'll go with you!"

"No, you will stay here. You'll wait ten minutes and then run off in a different direction."

"Are you abandoning me?"

"No, I'm going to lead those people away from the warehouse."

"Please don't abandon me!"

"You must understand, Anaid." Old Aramais passed his hand tenderly over the girl's face. "You must remain alive to tell my son all about it later. His name is Arshik. Agreed?"

The girl said nothing.

"Only don't come out immediately, but wait until they are all running after me."

From the depths of the cellar came the sound of the ceiling falling in with a crash, and a column of flame shot up from the old school building. The crowd could feel the heat. The door of the warehouse opened slowly and old Aramais appeared with a revolver in his hand.

"There he is!" came the cry from the crowd. The little boys let out penetrating whistles. Then the young men wielding iron bars rushed at him. Aramais raised his revolver and fired over their heads. The boys backed off. Aramais fired again, this time at their feet. They broke into a run. The crowd joined them in retreating. No one wanted to risk their lives because of some old Armenian.

Aramais realized that he must not let such a moment pass, and he ran off in the other direction. The first to notice this were the little boys, for whom everything that was happening was just an amusing spectacle. They whistled and jeered after him.

The crowd came gradually to a halt, and, now even more angry because of the humiliating fear it had displayed when confronted by one man, rushed after Aramais.

He was running with some difficulty down the street towards the Armenian cemetery. He had chosen that way subconsciously because it was there that Susana was buried. It was there that a modest gravestone stood, with her photograph mounted in it. It showed Susana as a young girl with laughing eyes, just as Aramais first saw her that day in Bulgaria.

It became more and more difficult for him to run—his age was showing. His heart was beating at such a rate that it seemed to be on the verge of bursting. But old Aramais kept running. Ever more slowly, but still running. He had to give the girl time to get well away from the warehouse. He knew that, once they had finished him off, the crowd would inevitably return to drag home the expensive tires from the shop.

The crowd caught up with him. It swept along the street in a dark howling mass, so that now only a machine gun could have stopped them. "I can't do any more," Aramais said hoarsely, and dropped into a walk. "I'm too old." He regained his breath, then turned, walked towards the crowd and raised his now useless revolver.

The first stone that was thrown made a bad cut in his forehead. Old Aramais staggered but stayed on his feet. That one was followed by a hail of stones. Aramais fell to his knees, then tried to rise, but the crowd of maddened people, with their hot breath smelling strongly of alcohol and sweat, trod him underfoot.

All this took place in the town of Sumgait, in the Soviet Socialist Republic of Azerbaijan, on the evening of Saturday, February 27, in the year 1988. It was three days before troops were finally brought in and the violent repression was brought to an end.

But there was an even more frightful and large-scale pogrom ahead for the Armenians in Baku, the capital of Azerbaijan. And outright war in Nagorno-Karabakh.